KIRKBY-IN-ASHFIELD

Yesterday Remembered

KIRKBY-IN-ASHFIELD

Yesterday Remembered

GERALD LEE

SUTTON PUBLISHING

First published in the United Kingdom in 2007 by
Sutton Publishing, an imprint of NPI Media Group Limited
Cirencester Road · Chalford · Stroud · Gloucestershire · GL6 8PE

British Library Cataloguing in Publication Data
A catalogue record for this book is available from the British Library.

ISBN 978-0-7509-4882-1

Typeset in 11.5/14pt Sabon.
Typesetting and origination by
NPI Media Group Limited.
Printed and bound in England.

Contents

Foreword

Yesterday Remembered? Those two words certainly opened the floodgates. So many memories, so many comparisons with life today. This is only to be expected when you have lived in one place practically all your life.

Take the population for instance: so different today from the time when Kirkby was mainly a mining area set amid much agriculture. Way back in my boyhood I was told the population was 7,000 covering East Kirkby and Kirkby-in-Ashfield, and then, with mining and increased railway activity over the next thirty years, the figure rose to around 17,000. Now, we no longer have mining (but nevertheless there has been an influx of people into the Kirkby area) and the 2002 population was already in excess of 25,000.

It is so difficult to pinpoint precisely how this happened. 'Well, I'll tell you how,' said a longstanding friend. 'It is the car that has done it. People can more or less choose where they want to live, make sure they have a car – or more than one – and they can use the place as a dormitory and work away from home.' Maybe he was right: very few pedestrians go past my window these days but there is an almost unending stream of cars.

Walking to the local shops was at one time an accepted part of life. Today it is a different story. of course there are people who take note of the need for exercise and do their stint of pedestrian shopping, but certainly not so many as there were in time gone by.

'Well,' said my old friend, 'one of the great differences is that the days you and I remember as children, having a car of your own was about as likely as winning the pools. And you didn't need your own transport because there were so many small shops here, there and everywhere.'

He had obviously given some thought to the way both Kirkbys were joined and have developed. 'Cars and television,' he said. 'If we hadn't those treasures think what a different place our town would be.' How right he is.

He started to walk away and then sharply turned back. 'Here, think about this,' he said. 'You don't see youngsters playing out in the streets as we used to, do you?' He didn't wait for an answer, but went on regardless. 'Can't expect them to, wouldn't be safe. And another thing. There are not so may local football and cricket teams, and sports field are often scarcely used,' He was obviously warming to his theory. 'I'll tell you what. Look out one of your old footballs. You were the sort of kid who always had a football. Find one and then we'll go up to the rec. I could just do with a kickabout! Eh, what about it?'

That was his parting shot before he toddled off down the road, now-bent shoulders gently shaking with laughter. He was always a humourist.

Gerald Lee, 2007

1

Gas Lamps & Candlesticks

When I think back to boyhood in Kirkby in the 1920s I remember the street lighting that provided areas of illumination and long patches of darkness. In winter the town was a much darker place than we know today.

The streets were lit by gas lamps and obviously the lamplighters couldn't be everywhere at the same time. We lived on Cookson Street and I can recall the lamplighter walking up the street carrying his long pole, with which he opened the glass side of the lamp, pulled down the chain inside and lit the gas mantle. And when he reappeared on the morning shift he was known, particularly in factory districts, to tap on assigned bedroom windows with his lighter pole. 'Come on, let's be having you. It's six o'clock and time you were making a move!' And a pint of beer might be his reward later in the week.

I was in my early teens before we had electric lighting and a clear memory is of seeing my mother standing on the living room table unhooking a ceiling plate hanging above the gas light to wash off the gas fumes. And, until electricity was installed, I never remember a fixed light in the bedrooms.

Here comes a candle to light you to bed – and the gas lamps you left downstairs.

How does the line in the old nursery rhyme go? 'Here comes a candle to light you to bed, and here comes a chopper to chop off your head'. No wonder the kids were frightened. Imagine hearing this while holding a candle and seeing those fantastic shapes the flickering flame threw up on the ceiling. People might laugh today, with modern amenities at the touch of a button, but childhood didn't necessarily link a spluttering candle with hilarity. Just as it never seemed to be a lot of fun starting the day washing the sleep out of your eyes from a tap over a stone sink with the water as cold as the winter morning.

Yet my grandfather seemed to revel in his icy ablutions. On the odd occasion I saw him performing his daily ritual, his muscular torso seeming to fill his tiny bathroom, out would come his usual proclamation: 'I might be an old man, but I don't want to be a dirty old man.' He smiled at the admiring small boy, who had heard from more than one of Grandad's contemporaries that there were not many who would willingly have tangled with him.

Grandad was a local character, one of many in the neighbourhood. It seems, looking back, there were more characters about then. Maybe because people did more walking and, as a consequence, you saw more of your neighbours. Plenty of buses and trains of course, but the days when you tripped off here, there and everywhere in your car was still a long way off. Kerbside conversation was an accepted fact of life.

Bobby Harris when he was awheel.

You even had a word or two with Bobby Harris, the School Attendance Officer. Bowler-hatted and gaitered, smallish and always in a grey suit, there had been days when he made you want to be as inconspicuous as possible. If you were home from school for any reason you could be sure it wouldn't be long before he would come pedalling down the street and knocking on the door. He was a kind enough man, but that bowler and his gaiters set him apart, and woe betide anyone who was away from school without good reason. The visit made, down would go your name in the little black book. Strictly a no-nonsense man operating in a no-nonsense time. But his visits could have a lighter side. He was never short of a remedy (or wemedy, favouring 'w' for 'r') if the nipper had been laid low by eating too many scrumped apples!

If Bobby Harris carried out his job with quiet precision, Jack Tatton did his (or one of them) with a noisy efficiency. Jack was, for many years, Kirkby's Town Crier. Whenever there were local events to be announced Jack was your lad. A mighty man, he always seemed to me, marching around to various vantage points in the district. Holding his large bell by the clapper not a sound was heard until he went into action, but when he did at some pre-arranged street corner you knew he was there. A dozen clangs on his bell, a brief pause, and then his remarkable voice made itself heard.

He told miners about meetings on Kirkby's famous Pondhole; he announced gatherings to be held in the Market Hall; he made you aware if

Jack Tatton, kneeling, chimney sweep and Town Crier, with friends and neighbours from Byron Street.

something special should be happening shortly in any corner of the parish. We lived more than fifty yards away from the spot he always chose at the corner of Park Street and Cookson Street and my father, instantly aroused from his Sunday afternoon slumber, had no difficulty in hearing Jack's every word, and was often tempted to reply with a few of his own. No traffic about to speak of then, of course, but ears were happily tuned in to those stentorian tones.

Jack was not only the Town Crier: he made his living as a chimney-sweep, never short of custom and sending out willing nippers and their mums to look for the magic brush appearing out of now much cleaner chimneys.

'My word', my mother would say, 'the chimney's pulling better.' And she meant it, just as Dad did when he tipped a good helping of soot on his rhubarb patch. 'That'll help make a good pie or two before we're much older,' he prophesied.

2

Yards of History

Church Street tells so much of Kirkby's story. As you walk along what is one of the most widely used thoroughfares of the town it is hard to visualise the changes that have taken place. Inevitably many of the old buildings have disappeared as has the level of activity in the street's daily shopping. What a hive of activity it always seemed to be, people going about their affairs and not having to be cooped up behind the high school wall, free to stride along the street and maybe make a call upon one of the many fascinating Yards.

You could bob into the Co-op to buy a bit of something for lunch. The gentleman who managed the store in those long lost days was Mr Bradshaw. A distinguished-looking man even in his white apron, whom we met many years later when we were at Sutton-on-Sea. He had retired to Trusthorpe and was then a churchwarden at the village church.

So much sticks in the mind even at a distance of more than seventy years. There were so many interesting shops. The smart little establishment at the top of Orchard Walk where I recall seeing displayed in its window hats, scarves, gloves and various patterns of material tastefully draped to attract the ladies.

It is hard now to imagine so many establishments vying for the hard-earned money of the residents. Let's think of one or two others. There was a fish and chip shop, and not far away from that was Bray's the furnishers. There was an estate agent shop at the end of Batemans Yard owned by E. and J. Lowe, who at the time collected many of the rents in the district (and surprisingly it was also the local tax office).

Wightman's post office was a lean-to attached to the building that housed the fruit and confectionery business – it did a thriving trade. Memory evokes the smell of that shop; always a pleasure to go in and remembered for having an uneven floor. I recall arranging to take a telephone call at the post office when I had to look after the office where I worked in Nottingham. My boss was on holiday at Mablethorpe (the firm was on short time and closed for a week) and he wanted to know if there

Wightman's post office, a one-time thriving business.

Built in 1738 this house was once a post office, too. It has recently been extensively rebuilt.

were any important letters he should know about. So Mr Wightman said I could arrange to take a call on his premises. An incident that underlines the scarcity of phones at that time in Kirkby.

But back to Church Street and its shops. You could buy newspapers, fish and chips, sweets, stamps, clothes, furniture, groceries, beer and wines, have your watches and clocks mended, get your hair cut and treat yourself to a delectable sandwich or home-made pastry. The old Kirkby population, which was considerable, was well catered for.

There was the occasional bus, but walking was the main method of getting about. Hardly surprising that two conveniently placed pubs were never short of trade. The Duke of Wellington has stood the test of time and still thrives. Years ago there was a large storehouse at the side of the Duke, and nailed to the wall fronting the street was a large metal plate informing anyone interested that it was 120 miles to London. At one time that would surely have fascinated any of Kirkby's budding Dick Whittingtons.

The Croft, originally built in the sixteenth century. It was once the town's lock-up. Here it is after much rebuilding.

The other public house was the Green Man (remembering Robin Hood said many of the locals) almost opposite to the entrance to Titchfield Park. The one-time popular hostelry was kept by Mr Herbert Beaumont who later (when the pub was demolished) went to live at Ash Farm on Sutton Road.

We cannot leave Church Street without mentioning the various clusters of cottages, known as yards. Each Yard bore the name of a well-known Kirkby resident, some dating back to the seventeenth century. There was Brunts Yard, Bradleys, Batemans, Davisons, Crees, Heaths and Sharleys, all tightly grouped about their communal entrances. The cottage amenities were crude by today's standards but many highly-regarded families lived in reasonable amity with their neighbours.

Kirkby Cross has been in situ since the thirteenth century. Beyond it can be seen Church Street.

At the south end of Church Street stood St Wilfrid's. Lovingly cared for down the centuries, the original building dated back to 1150. In 1907 it was grievously damaged by fire; the only parts left relatively undamaged were the tower and the spire. But by superhuman effort the church was reopened for worship on 7 November 1908. Although rebuilt on the lines of the old building, there were a number of additions, all crafted and installed after much consideration and overseen by Mr Louis Ambler, the architect largely responsible for the restoration. St Wilfrid's stands today at the summit of Church Hill overlooking much of the local countryside.

It is fitting that, at the north end of Church Street, stands the Market Cross. It was in 1261 that a charter for a market and fair was granted to the old village, and it seems appropriate that the ancient street has weathered its storms and prospered in an interesting stretch between cross and church.

3

Gentlemen & Players

When you met Sam Davies – if you were a sportsman – there was never any shortage of conversation. His terrier, boon companion when he retired, knew it had to content itself until its master gave the word to move on. Sam is still missed by many of those who knew him. His sporting memories were prodigious; chiefly they were about local football and cricket. You could be sure that the tales he told and the incidents he and his companions recalled, were never far from Kirkby. More than likely they were closer to Nuncargate.

Kirkby LMS FC, 1947. Sam Davies stands, hands on hips, in the back row.

Nuncargate CC. Sam Davies is seated second from the right on the front row.

In the years just before and after the Second World War there was an abundance of local sporting talent and, although kinship to one's own club was always applauded, a man could be encouraged to display his prowess with other teams should the occasion arise, particularly at football. Sam's ability was well known and he would never go short of a game. The photograph on page 9 shows him in the Kirkby LMS team soon after the war was over and more peaceful contests beckoned.

But it must be said that club loyalty gained a favourable mark at cricket and nowhere more so than Nuncargate. Small wonder; it had a tradition going back many years and had in its time encouraged some of the most honoured names in the game. No club could ask for more illustrious players than Larwood and the Hardstaffs! It was no surprise that when the statue of Harold Larwood was placed in Kirkby Precinct, the importance of the Nuncargate ground was not forgotten. The new pavilion will forever be linked with the great fast bowler and his youthful companions. And a visit to the popular Cricketers' Arms, a few yards away, will always bring you in contact with someone able to recall the sporting exploits of an earlier age.

So it will be well understood that Sam, when his days as an employee of Ashfield District Council had ended, proved to be an enduring character with many a story to tell of former days of glory.

There was a proliferation of playing pieces, both for football and cricket, dotted about the Kirkby area in the days before and after the last war, but if the Nuncargate ground had special memories for so many people, so did the sporting complex at one time part and parcel of Bentinck Colliery's amenities. Neatly laid out behind a wall bordering Sutton Road, there were areas for football (and some memorable matches were played there), tennis and bowls. But it was the cricket ground that witnessed some of the greatest of Kirkby's sporting days. The wicket and outfield had long been in the hands of Arthur Huften; the playing pieces he prepared were appreciated, not only by local players, but by countless teams who graced the ground in that halcyon period in the early 1930s and resumed after Hitler was vanquished.

The lovely Bentinck ground still stands, mostly deserted these days, but always looking ready to accommodate talent and enthusiasm. No-one better could have been found to write of happier days than George Shacklock, one

George Shacklock and wicket-keeper Len Whyld ready for action beside Mr Shacklock Snr.

George Shacklock on active service, 1943.

of the best of Bentinck captains, schoolmaster, wartime naval officer and tremendous enthusiast. He wrote to me:

The club in the 1920s was, of course, Kirkby Portland. As a schoolboy I remember the thrill of playing against their 2nd XI on that marvellous pitch. I think Jack Baker took the captaincy through the transition which changed its character, and later I took over from him. Dear old Fred Hall maybe took over when I left to go to the war after being skipper for ten years.

You were very right about the depth of the talent available. I remember managing to get three 50s in a row under the benign and very rotund Kenneth Logan to get into the 1st XI from the second team. Reg Lester led the batting order while Ernie Marshall sustained the attack with his marvellous classic action, which Ron Allin mirrored in later years. It was a happy day when Reg Lester and I each had a century in a cup-tie against Shirebrook.

As young players we benefitted enormously from the ready encouragement and equally caustic criticism from the experts who sat in the seats in front of the pavilion. These included Sam and Dick Lowe whose professional migrations to South Wales did so much to bring the Glamorgan County Cricket Club to eventual first-class status.

This era saw the introduction of limited-overs cricket for evening games, and I can still feel the ball on the bat while reaping 94 in eighteen overs on the tiny Nuncargate ground, from where I hasten to add Lol Larwood had earlier departed to higher encounters with the county and England.

Many local people will recall the opening of the Simpson, Wright and Lowe sports ground along Sutton Road in a snowstorm at the end of April; a representative district side entertained the County XI, and we had a blizzard while fielding!

A word about Ron Allin, the gentle giant with the perfect action. He perished in one too many raids on the submarine pens at St Nazaire, leaving his wife and two boys. No finer sportsman went on to the field, and he bowled his heart out for me on many occasions.

But like all fast bowlers he liked to get runs as well, and one day on the Huthwaite ground we were nine down for 69 when Ron came in to join me. Suddenly, forgetting all the theory of batting he launched into the attack and sent the ball into all the vacant places. The innings closed at 165, and that tenth-wicket stand must still be a record.

The scorebooks that recorded those happy days were kept by Charlie Badham. I wonder if they were passed on to his daughter Rosa? A name that I wouldn't want to be missing from my team is Oz Hart. He was my stock bowler, a cheerful soul who glared like Freddie Trueman at any batsman who successfully fended off a seamer which threatened to break his hip bone.

Looking back I must say that the rot had already set in during the late 1930s. The standards of ability were beginning to drop. In spite of the vastly superior conditions of accommodation and pitches the influx of young cricketers seemed to die away. Was it because we no longer produced the Barratt, the Staples, the Larwood, the Voce, the Hardstaffs – great players a youngster could set his sights on? Was it because the village clubs died? Or was it that not enough youngsters were given the right sort of encouragement in a rapidly changing world?

We shall never know, George, we shall never know. But one thing is for sure. If they had looked they couldn't have set their sights on a better example than the man who skippered the old Bentinck Colliery team with such distinction.

4

Before the Car Was King & Now

For countless years Kirkby was rural and seemed destined to stay that way. Wherever you were within its boundaries you were never far away from fields, a few trees or valuable agricultural land. But over time there have been changes; the rural air has largely disappeared. Three factors have featured heavily in the town's development.

The first was the change in the local industrial scene with the closure of the mines in both Kirkby and the surrounding district. The road I live

East Kirkby looking along ancient Kingsway. It was then named Cemetery Road.

Kingsway, no longer East Kirkby, at a somewhat later date then the photograph at the bottom of page 15.

in is a pretty good example of the difference the closure of the Summit Colliery made to certain parts of the town. It is going back a bit now of course to the days when the only major activity hereabouts was the miners going to or returning from the mine a mile away.

The postal address of the road is still 'lane', widened and resurfaced over the years from tamped-down earth to well-maintained macadam. Miners trudged by in their scores, pit-blackened and with steel-shod boots clanking on the hard road that the lane eventually became. The only wheeled traffic were the colliery lorries, the very occasional car and motorcycle, and a fair number of well-worn bikes.

Across the lane were fields and gardens, and at most times from spring to early winter you could reckon on seeing miners who rented the allotments catching what light there was to tend their plots and, in due time, returning home with their vegetable- and flower-laden barrows. Colliers were truly gardeners *par excellence*, always eager to work their space after long hours below ground. Doubtless it was the freedom they felt when they reached the surface that heightened their enthusiasm for the clean air denied them during much of their working life.

Low Moor Road with traffic lights in place.

The Four Lane Ends. Note the white line signifying 'major road ahead'.

Station Street, photographed in the 1970s.

Pure nostalgia: Kirkby level crossing.

The second thing that had a major effect on Kirkby was the abolition of the railway crossing gates at the west end of Station Street in 1971/2. When they were removed and the rails taken up there was speculation and jubilation – the latter for motorists as a great source of irritation had gone.

Those crossing gates had for years been the bane of road travellers, causing much bad temper and blue language. The whoops of joy from motorists when the line was closed following the Beeching Report could have been heard throughout the district. One form of transport gave hope for another much more convenient and quicker way of travelling.

Many of those who gave three cheers at the demise of the railways have no doubt realised (those who are still travelling and who remember how things once were) how little inconvenience we had to endure compared with today. The situation now is that we have infinitely more traffic on the roads and a railway system that is nothing like as efficient as the one we once had.

And the third major factor? The replanning of the routes into and out of our growing town. As someone said to me one day: 'It's like trying to get six fingers into a five-fingered glove.' And that, to someone who uses the town regularly, must seem to be near enough what it is like with the increase of traffic lights at short distances, and what is often insufficient time to make real progress when your 'green for go' is of extremely brief duration. And the problems are made worse by the immense increase in the town's motor traffic.

'But it's the same everywhere,' an old schoolfriend said. 'You ought to take a walk down any of the side streets.' He waved his arm in a long sweep. 'Try any of them and you'll see what I mean.'

So I did and, naturally enough, chose the street where I had spent my boyhood years. It is a street that had served us well enough and is remembered with affection. I didn't move from it until I was twenty-four and just married. It was a haven when I came home on leave during the Second World War. Hardly a motorised vehicle to be seen in those days, simply a 1940s extension of what I knew from my youth.

The street had two parlour-shops. Deliveries were made a few times a week, not often enough to stop our unending street games. Those games were often tied to the calendar, but nothing hard and fast. The only requirement was to have enough light after school and at weekends to show your expertise at whip and top (Shrove Tuesday for that), football and cricket, skipping (mainly a girls' game, of course) that called for running into a rope that stretched from one pavement to the other. And

Cookson Street, typical of so many residential streets today. Only expert parkers need apply!

games of hide and seek, marbles, fag-cards (skimming yours against an opponent's set up against a wall), hopscotch, tin lurky. And if darkness came down suddenly, Dick, Dick, Shine a Light.

Traffic? Deliveries to the shops and perhaps an emergency call from a doctor. But little else. And now? I couldn't believe it. In the 200-odd yards from one end to the other there were, when I walked the length of the street the first time in a long while, forty-four cars and one van parked tight to the pavements.

A quick trip to another half-dozen streets proved my old friend was right. Cars had been skilfully parked in every conceivable space, bumper to bumper. Now, truly it can be said, the car is king.

How different it was in 1959, the year I bought my first car. It was a Ford Popular, a grand little roadster that took four of us (and often five) to distant places in our great country. The price? £295, bumped up to a hefty £443 17s (don't forget the shillings) when the tax was added. Three forward gears and, driven with care and attention, 40 miles to the gallon. It only had two doors, but once our three adults and two boys were installed there was room enough. And, wrote an eminent motoring journalist at the time, there was plenty of headroom for the so-inclined proud owner to wear his top hat! What a car!

But, as ever in the Kirkby of that time, there were lynx-eyed policemen awheel, and on one memorable workday morning, as I approached our local Shoulder of Mutton Hill hoping the Popular would take the steep incline smoothly on the near-deserted road, I was stopped by one such policeman and told: 'I have followed you for the last mile, sir, and twice your speed has reached thirty-two miles per hour. I am warning you this time, but if I have to speak to you again there will be trouble.' I thanked him profusely, carefully wound up my window and went gently on my almost solitary way.

5

Sunshine & Siberia

The walk to the top of Diamond Avenue had been worthwhile, especially when we paused to breathe easily again. This particular day when we reached the top the early morning clouds had disappeared and the sun was shining out of a winter sky, a real transformation. Nail Nest Hill, we were always told at junior school, was 636ft above sea level, and as you looked back over Kirkby you could well believe it.

As we stood there I found myself recalling a day when I had my father as companion. I was twelve years old and a remark he made then has remained crystal clear.

A fine winter morning at the top of Nail Nest Hill.

'Now, that car there,' he said as a shiny black saloon came over the hill, 'is described as the leader of light cars.'

That astonished me. The year was 1934, and I should think my dad wouldn't have been in a car more than a handful of times in his life. I could just imagine him sitting there and being ready to hop out at the slightest stuttering of the engine. As far as he was concerned a car was a box of tricks, and not all of them were reliable.

I still have his yearbook and it describes on a full page advertisement the 8HP Ford, a saloon de luxe, with a choice of two doors (price £120) or four doors (price £145). And there is a nice touch that says: 'From places nearly as far apart as the Poles, every post brings messages of cordial appreciation of "The Leader of Light Cars".'

'The Leader of Light Cars': the 8HP Ford.

The morning was a happy recollection of a fine man still recovering from miners' nystagmus, and I found myself recalling another thing he had told me as a schoolboy, again standing at the top of Nail Nest Hill.

He didn't say whether he had rode up the hill, or whether he had needed to push his bike up and then get riding. But he did say: 'Yes, my old boneshaker took me on some good journeys. From here I rode to Newark, and most of the time we were on roads little better than cart-tracks.'

That bike must have been a good one. A Sunbeam if I remember rightly, that Father said he had bought for £14. Now that was a sum that must have been an absolute fortune in his biking days. And it showed a bit of enterprise, a happy memory to dwell on, and entirely appropriate now that the sun really was shining.

It is difficult, when you are in the sunlight, to brood upon dark thoughts. You must have noticed that of course. Odd bits of gloom are dispelled, and surely even the most confirmed pessimist must feel all is not lost while we can be sure of sunshine now and then.

It is a different tale when rain is pelting the pavements. The man up the road who, on brighter days, is willing to discuss anything from spring cabbage to the winsome smile of the latest television charmer, is turned into a glowering individual barely acknowledging you from under the brim of his dripping hat.

The dainty little woman who serves cups of tea so engagingly at the church functions takes on a fresh personality, threatens young James as he springs from puddle to puddle, and addresses burly tradesmen who have forgotten some unimportant items in phrases harsh enough to send them scurrying back to their vans.

But it is the wind that plays havoc with tempers. When a vicious gust whips a sheet off the clothes-line and carries it over the hedge in the manner of an Oriental carpet, you can, if you are a humorist and if your washing machine is in particularly good form – laugh until the windows shake.

But if, despite all entreaties, you have stuck to the virtues of the washtub, it is more than likely that an innocent husband will have it laid at his door that he wants to see his wife turned into a slave as she struggles with a soiled sheet.

It is the husband's turn if the sweetpea canes are blown down or the favoured chrysanths are snapped off. Then all the cats and dogs in the neighbourhood are in mortal peril.

Snow? Ah yes, snow has an effect all of its own. When it comes we know the worst of winter has arrived and it is treated as a common enemy – by adults anyway. It is fought with combined resources. Mother puts Father's slippers to warm, and there is sharp concern over the cost of fuel. The mining fraternity were once of course in the fortunate position of having their concessionary loads of coal. The children, always keen to make the most of white adventure, are given Mr Leatherland's cold preventatives and wrapped in extra scarves.

'We must take care,' Mother says anxiously. 'It's all right Mother Goose shaking her feathers, but now she's let us know she is still there, the sooner she packs up the better.'

When the first two months have been torn off the calendar, though, jauntiness in the stride and crocuses in the borders indicate better days are on their way.

Better weather? That, assuming there is good weather and bad, is the whole nub of the matter. Of course, there is good and bad local weather (the folk who live in Nottingham always say that Kirkby is a topcoat colder than they are used to) but if we could arrange universal good weather maybe we would see a whole new approach to international living spring up overnight.

Think of it this way: climate has quite an influence upon people, be they postmen or politicians. When you snuggle under yor blankets on a winter night, it's all Downing Street to a hot-water bottle the Prime Minister is doing the same. For humans are humans when all is said and done.

And that, perhaps, is why it is easy to wipe the sunny grin off the face of a visiting African dignitary if he is met by the chill of an English March. As he shares the conference table with a clutch of other delegates, and maybe still thinking of his home in sunnier climes, we get a headline on our breakfast table the next day that is as full of tension as a panther's spring.

Similarly, could we really expect a delegate who lives a short ride from Vladivostok to give of his diplomatic best at a meeting held within perspiring distance of the Equator?

Maybe it all boils down (or freezes up) to blood cells, predestination, or simply a harsh Mother Nature; but the fact remains that one man's paradise can easily be another man's prison. One wonders if what we in England consider sweet reason is simply the result of living in a climate that is either as fussy as lavender and old lace or as frozen as an old brass monkey.

Deep thoughts indeed, but perhaps the top of Nail Nest Hill is as good a place to have them as anywhere.

6

Treasure Box

Cleaning out a cupboard brought the box to light. It had lain there for a forgotten number of years; no doubt it had been subjected to much dusting, but the lid had remained shut. Now it was knocked out of place and there was a sudden cascade of colour. In a moment scores of reminders of a vanished schoolboy age lay scattered on the carpet.

Turn the clock back and it could have been a long-ago day when Robert was aloft, snug, and probably dreaming of a jet aircraft he had seen that morning streaking across the summer sky. In a flash I had added a year or two to his age, assumed his cap and short trousers, and was on my knees among the treasure that will one day be handed to him with becoming ceremony.

There they lay, close on five hundred cigarette cards, a collection built up by persistent badgering of my elders and expanded by much shrewd bargaining among my contemporaries.

I remembered the pang of disappointment when a greatly coveted card passed into hands as eager as my own and only because I could not produce the particular number out of 'Great Ships' that was the exchange demanded. But what joy when the remaining card to make up the set of 'Old London' was smilingly handed to me by a man who wore a coat with an astrakhan collar. A man of obvious substance.

A glance at the carpet now and I was able to nod again at the heroes of my youth. There they were, gloriously captured forever on pieces of highly-coloured card. Walter Hammond, majestically depicted among a set of 'Champions', his flashing blade raised at the end of a sizzling cover-drive; Larwood, on the point of hammering his left foot down into the summer turf; Duckworth, for once without his famous white hat that accompanied his vociferous 'Owzat?'.

Footballers too. Here was Ted Ditchburn. 'He makes the hardest saves seem ordinary. Perhaps the best custodian since Frank Swift', says the legend on the reverse of his picture. And then there are two of the greatest-

ever Manchester United players: 'Busby Babes' Jacky Blanchflower and
Duncan Edwards. How much heartache there is simply to remember them.
How those three great players would have enhanced the wizardry of any
era in which they played.

William T. Tilden

Mrs. Helen Wills-Moody

Miss Betty Nuthall

H. W. Austin

A set of boxers lay tumbled into one illustrious heap; Len Johnson was there, so was Harvey the supreme, Carnera, Kid Lewis. Their records, cold enough in yesterday's print, were full of meaning again after half an hour in their sepia-coloured presence.

Jockeys, racing motorists, wizards of Wimbledon. Ah yes, there was a set that devotees of the Centre Court would revel in – Helen Wills-Moody, Betty Nuthall, H.W. Austin, Bill Tilden – conjuring up memories of long-past triumphs.

But the collection was never intended to be a concentration of sporting giants. There was a set of 'Animals and Their Furs', lovely illustrations that would have been useful to any teacher. There were 'Famous British Liners' to warm a sailor's heart. And the large, lovely cards showing 'Beautiful Homes' from Stirlingshire to Kent.

'Arms of the British Empire', 'Modern Architecture', 'Old London'. And, to bring us back to sport again: 'Famous Golfers' – James Braid, Walter Hagen, Edward Ray, a great triumvirate from the elect.

What a pity that My Lady Nicotine was so heavily involved!

7

Ancient Encounter

It was a beautiful Saturday morning, more so because I was off to watch a day's cricket at Nottingham. Kirkby looked placid under the blue sky. And so it should: the war was over, and now all efforts could be turned to what we all hoped would be peace and prosperity.

Happy thoughts, and taken with me from my local bus to the trolleybus I transferred to in Nottingham. It was a good feeling and because I am not the most unsociable of men I spoke to the Ancient gent who shared my seat. I murmured pleasantly: 'Nice to see the sun, don't you think?'

The Ancient gripped the seat in front with a bony hand and waited while the trolleybus negotiated a particularly busy bit of Arkwright Street before he turned two penetrating blue eyes upon me, starting at my top waistcoat button, flitting on to my tie, and coming to rest on eyes that wilted not a little.

'And don't you think it should be sunny, this time of year?' he demanded in a hostile tone. His bowtie was fidgeted by a frisky Adam's apple.

The sun was hot and strong. Breakfast had been a happy meal of bacon and egg. There was a county match at Trent Bridge. I was almost sorry I had been sociable.

I looked at the pale blue eyes again. 'Yes,' I muttered, 'I suppose really. I mean I have known it to be . . .'

The bowtie jumped, and the ancient gathered his forces. 'Of course you have. Everybody has,' he said, with telepathic assurance. And then it started. 'When I was a youngster we were having better weather than this in March. Why! I've been out in the country on a spring day with no more on than a pocket-handkerchief. Weather! This isn't weather. It should be boiling!'

Whether it was the sun, the heating system on our bus, or merely the fire of the Ancient's words I don't know, but I was sweating.

We lurched round on to the Embankment and scrambled off the bus. I turned on the Ancient what I hoped was a friendly parting smile. I might just as well have smiled at a frozen cod.

Ace fast-bowler Harold Larwood meets King George V.

A Nottinghamshire team even the Ancient must have approved of! Harris, Sam Staples, Voce, Hardstaff, Arthur Staples, Larwood, G.V. Gunn, Walker, Keeton, A.W. Carr (Captain), George Gunn, Lilley.

'Going there?' he demanded, his stick pointing at the green-and-gold flag of an illustrious cricket club. I nodded. 'So am I,' he said, and, as a qualification: 'Only because there's nothing better to do!'

At the turnstiles I produced my ticket. I hoped hard, but the Ancient was a member too. There was colour in the crowd and warmth in the wooden seats. 'Not a bad ground,' ceded the Ancient. 'Lovely,' I said, grateful for that spark of approval. The runs were coming easily, and I said so.

'Aye, and so they should. This isn't bowling; it's playing at it. They want somebody who can whip 'em down.'

Suddenly a stump was knocked back and a bail flew. That, surely, was one to me.

'Ha! Batting! Where are the batsmen?' the Ancient tilted his hat menacingly over his eyes. 'Where are the Graces, the Gilbert Jessops?'

Women say the quickest way to a man's heart is through his stomach. I tried liquid refreshment on the Ancient. He accepted my glass and drank deeply. For a moment his eyes were thoughtful. I permitted myself an inward chuckle. 'And they have the cheek,' he said dreamily, 'to call this beer. When I was younger, two glasses and you'd have been standing on your head.'

I didn't say anything, but standing on my head has never been one of my accomplishments. I paid for another drink. The Ancient's denunciation of present-day beer increased in violence. It was bad enough to attract the attention of another man who, in less than three minutes, had become as a brother to my aged companion.

Thankfully I slipped away, vowing that when old age comes I shall tell the youngsters a thing or two. If their beer and cricket are weaker than ours they are in for a high old time and no mistake.

But steady on, Kirkby is a territory to tread carefully. Beer and cricket – and tradition is there to prove it – in this proud old community have never been noticeably lacking in strength.

8

The Clinging Vine

O f all enthusiasts there can be few more capable of infecting other people than gardeners. Mention slugs and they know how to guard against them. Talk of pruning and a pocket knife will appear like magic, to be followed by a demonstration regardless of time or venue. Ask for advice and you will find yourself loaded with books, catalogues and practical information guaranteed to turn you into a horticulturist in no time.

When I casually mentioned grapevines (I was still in my twenties, living in a great gardening area, and keen to become green-fingered) I had plunged unwittingly down a road of unknown length. My friend stopped working, cleared a piece of his bench, and produced a stick of chalk. With more enthusiasm than artistry there was a drawing on the cleared space. 'Now, suppose this is your vine.' A gnarled finger indicated the tortuous lines of chalk. I nodded, assuming an interest I found hard to sustain.

For half-an-hour the instruction continued. I had been taken over the first year of growth, and the second, and was well into the third. I was growing more grapes than I could reasonably cope with and attaining a popularity among admiring neighbours that the growing of tomatoes and hollyhocks had never achieved.

The outcome was that my instructor tapped my chest with his finger and, with the air of a benefactor, said he would let me have a vine. What, I asked, would it cost? 'I'll give it to you,' he said.

At home I was silent. They are suspicious of my new ventures, and were doubly so in my young manhood. Moreover I nourished a secret hope that my gardener friend would say no more and the vine subject would be allowed to shrivel and die.

Transport was another problem. My travelling was in those days done by bus, and in fourteen miles a vine might be responsible for all sorts of unpredictable things. Supposing an infant were to sit on its mother's knee in the seat next to mine. It might grab the vine and, with a seraphic smile, hand a portion to its mother. I could probably stop the child, but that

Bill Brownhill, at home with any aspect of gardening, was the temporary keeper of the vine. (See also page 57)

might cause a commotion, and I should be looked upon as a man who values a vine's growth more than an infant's happiness.

I could put it on the floor of the bus, but that would force me to sit in such a position as to make it look as if I suffered from arthritis.

Perhaps it could be placed in that dark recess under the stairs; but it was quite likely that the conductor would spot it and, pointing at my plant, enquire in stentorian tones: 'And where is this going?' And I was not particularly keen to answer that question.

But on the day the plant arrived I had a brainwave. I would send it by train – alone. Walking through the city I tried to look as much like a horticulturist as possible, stepping out briskly to discourage conversation and to show how well I could handle my burden.

The clerk at the station looked at me quizzically. 'Going to trust us with that?' he asked. 'Oh, it will be all right,' I said, as if sending vines by rail was my sole occupation. With a wave of my hand I left him to it.

During the day I brightened. So far all had gone well. Ours was a quiet station in those less frantic days, and I would be able to call for the plant, sneak up the lane, and have it in the greenhouse with nobody the wiser.

I had tea and went to collect the vine. I was feeling almost jaunty. And then it happened. The vicar was standing inside the booking office. His eyes were on the plant. He was talking to the clerk in a cultured undertone. Four eyes slowly turned upon me. The vicar beamed. 'Ah' he said, 'I see from the label that this is yours.' The beam broadened. 'I'm no hand with vines myself, but I wondered if you'd care to give us a lecture at our Wednesday get-together. You would make the whole thing fascinating I'm sure.'

9

Sound Advice

Old JGD was fond of saying 'You should have made a note of it at the time . . . That is the best way of remembering.' Certainly that was the case with what follows. The notes were written in October 1962 and they bring back a different world. Most assuredly headmaster JGD, now many years gone, his heavy eyebrows twitching, would have agreed with that.

There is no doubt about it. Walk into a house that has no television and you are at once aware that something is missing. The effect is about the same as being offered water to drink at an infantry reunion.

But television sets are no longer status symbols. 'Oh really?' as Aunt Cynthia once said, 'well, we changed our fourteen-inch for a twenty-one. They're in the room with you as you might say. Richard Dimbleby, Herbert said, smacked his lips when I put the cheese and pickles on the table.'

No, the size of the screen doesn't seem to matter now.

But the telly is, size notwithstanding, a compulsive piece of furniture. Even when it is off it stands there like a large blind eye. Forlorn, perhaps, when it is simply reflecting the contents of the room; and that must have been the feeling of the gentleman about whose son said to me: 'Dad's all right. It's a bit early in the day but there'll be a line or two to look at until the programme comes on.'

Maybe that old boy was something a bit more than a mere addict, but how often now does our conversation begin, or continue after a lull, 'Did you see. . .?'

But is it all lost, this mole-like existence a lot of us get caught up in? There were two ladies sitting behind me on the bus. Stuck close to a hedge at one point of the journey was a notice announcing a 'Young Farmers Ploughing Match.'

'A ploughing match, Gert? What's one o' them?'

You might have been excused for thinking Gert wouldn't have known. But she did, and explained it to her friend; finishing by pointing out, 'I saw 'em do an outside broadcast from one down in – where was it? – Essex, I think.'

It seems the real danger can best be summed up in the rather tired phrase of familiarity breeding contempt. If we had to be content with, say, an hour or so per day we might realise a bit more keenly how much we owe to John Logie Baird. But when a turn of the knob might take you to Wembley and football, or half-way round the world with adventurous spirits in the Peruvian Andes, you are inclined to ignore the technicalities involved.

But the real wonder seems to be – in television as with most other things – in the world of childhood. They, at least, are really living with the images on the tiny screen. But are they more entranced than we were with magic lanterns? Yes and no; no and yes: all such things are reduced (or enlarged) by the common denominator of childhood.

One thing occurs, though: will children become less adept in the art of conversation? For was there ever a better place to enrich one's thought than across the dining-table, merely through the cut and thrust of talk over Saturday high tea or Sunday dinner? But now it seems a great many meals are hurriedly eaten off the coffee-table in a semi-darkened room.

And are we more critical or gullible as a result of viewing? It all depends. 'I say, Glad, did you see . . . ?' 'Well, George, it said on the telly that. . .'

But at least television has taught one rather plump middle-aged lady something about ploughing matches, and it is quite on the cards she has been taught a good deal more since then.

It has been the cry for a long time now that we are becoming a nation of lookers instead of doers. Well, perhaps we are, but such sweeping generalisations are usually unreliable. Time marches on, and maybe it is simply a case of 'fings ain't wot they used to be'.

But shall we, one wonders, express dissatisfaction in the foreseeable future unless our accommodation, home or away, has all the modern conveniences, including a television in each room?

'I've set the alarm for one o'clock dear. They're televising the match from the moon. And I wouldn't like to miss Stanley Matthews. Not that he's finished mind you. I mean he's only fifty-three.'

The immortal Stanley Matthews.

Hardly in Sir Stanley's class!

'Ah, Stanley Matthews,' JGD might have said, 'a true and wonderful sportsman. Yes yes, you boys must see him.' And then: 'But our game starts in the big field at eleven o'clock sharp. Now don't forget that. In fact, make a note of it now. Before you leave your desks.'

10

A Lane That Turned

There is no better way to trace the way things once were on Southwell Lane than to start from the junction of Chapel Street, from Cookson House, still as foursquare as the day it was built. On your left as you walk along the pavement is a long stretch of grass favoured by short-cutters and dog walkers. They wouldn't have done that at one time as the land once steeped sharply to the busy LNER line that carried countless passenger and goods trains between north Nottinghamshire and Nottingham Victoria each day.

The Summit Colliery seen from Southwell Lane shortly after the Second World War. Speeds' Farm is on the left of the photograph.

The approach to Chapel Street with the path cutting across the field filled in over the one-time railway.

On the right, up to Cookson Street, are buildings that have, in recent years, housed printing, textile and engineering firms to add to Kirkby's enterprise; now, with the emphasis on car repairers, commercial endeavour continues.

But seventy years ago there was Scotherns Removals close by the corner house, mightily busy every day apart from Sunday. The Sabbath saw the doors tightly shut because the family were ardent Baptists, regular attenders at the little place of worship that stood next to the school on the appropriately named Chapel Street.

Scotherns had adequate transport in those sparsely-motorised days, with one vehicle particularly worthy of mention. It was a huge solid-tyred van certain to protect whatever goods were transported, but with a curious arrangement that left the much-valued driver very close to the elements. Fine in good weather, but not the place to be if it was raining. Protection could be found behind the windscreen, but a sort of mackintosh improvisation was put in place at the sides.

Where the Scothern premises stopped the Martin factory began. George Martin and his wife, Baptists like the Scotherns, were sweet manufacturers.

Southwell Lane now, but the colliery no longer exists.

Between them and an expanding workforce the business flourished and soon acquired a reputation for first-class confectionery. How well I remember in those early days seeing on Taunton railway station a large advert proclaiming to the travelling public: 'Martins Buttermints, Prince of Peppermints'. Eventually Martins moved to a splendid new factory a few hundred yards away, the firm's reputation assured.

In those days Southwell Lane was little more than a country track, tarmacked to make it easier travelling for the very occasional lorry and the very, very occasional car. From Cookson Street corner to fifty yards beyond the Hartley Road turning there were forty houses and a bungalow, all on the same side of the road as the factories. They were houses of some distinction in those days; there were not many families back then that could afford the few hundred pounds layout to build in such a quiet select area.

Among the families living on the lane were the Davisons (Daddy Davison was the name by which the old headmaster was affectionately known), Vernon White and his family (Vernon was an orthodontist in much demand) and, a bit further along, the Atkin family.

There is now much commercial enterprise leading off Southwell Lane.

Looking in the opposite direction, with the Orchid public house on the right.

Danny Atkin was one of the really good gardeners in the area, judging at countless shows after many years of winning prizes. Opposite his house at the corner of Bannerman Road was his allotment garden, a dozen strides from his front door.

This is where we really have to acknowledge the existence of allotments which at one time stretched all the way along one side of the road to Speeds' Farm almost half a mile away. It would be well-nigh impossible now to say just how many allotment gardens there were, but certainly the number would run into many dozens. And they weren't there simply for the tenants' pleasure and exercise; the produce that was trundled homewards in due season helped fill the cooking pots. But exercise and pleasure did come into it; maybe it was because they spent so much time underground that gave the miners such impetus. There was always keen rivalry at the local shows and immense pride when the judges had marked your carrots, beetroot or potatoes as winning exhibits.

There was just one break on the way down to Speeds' Farm, and that was a wide cart road that led to more allotments and the splendid new council estate. The road now, as it has been for many years, is Rowan Drive, but was then called, certainly by the old-timers, Sutton Middle Lane, offering a vigorous walk to our neighbouring town.

Speeds' Farm, at the right time of the year, was a place plenty of local lads made for. Potato-picking was the attraction and the regulars made sure they were in good time for acceptance. The pay wasn't generous by today's standards perhaps but it was more than a bit useful if you wanted to earn a few extra coppers.

But you had to work, and the chap who made make sure you got on with the job was Bill Speed, son of the old farmer who was now shrunken after a lifetime in the fields. But there was nothing shrinking about Bill. He was a big man, and when he raised his arms sideways you were looking at a man who had pretty well the biggest arm-stretch in the area. He was the sort of man you would think twice before tackling, and then decide it was more than your life was worth.

He was a cheerful enough chap when things were going well and you had listened to his instructions. 'Right you lads, heads down, bums up, and keep going'. And what did you get for your efforts? Well, strong empty bags were provided, and when you had filled one to Bill's satisfaction you were rewarded with sixpence. But sixpence was not to be sneezed at and you thought Speeds' Farm would go on forever.

But it didn't. There came a day when, instead of farming being the work that kept the fields looking good, and making the old farmhouse look so

Many of the rugby team were Welshmen who came to the area to work at the Summit Colliery. Their ground was a field close to Speeds' Farm.

attractive from a distance, the rural endeavours were gradually supplanted by loads of metal. The farm field was turned into a scrapyard, the house itself often scarcely visible from the lane.

Much was to change in the vicinity and in due time the rugby-playing Welsh miners who had sought work in the local mines in 1926 had to find somewhere else to pursue their sport. For a long time the rugby goalposts did duty on farm land. But one thing was for sure, they couldn't have been erected on the area adjacent to the farm.

I never heard much said about the rocky outcrop that must have been there for countless years. The Grand Canyon some of us christened it, and my curiosity was never satisfied. Stretching for over a hundred yards was this stone outcrop of varying height, an enticing place to be for exuberant lads. It was ideal for playing Cowboys and Indians, with the warhoops reverberating and the whoopers remaining hidden. It was a pretty spectacular place. When it was removed, and how, I never knew, but certainly I remember it well.

Beyond the Grand Canyon was a hill in the road, still there today, and beyond that were the headstocks of the noted Summit Colliery. The Summit, as we all called it, had a great reputation for its output. As long as

I could remember there were times during the day, obviously when it was a shift changeover, when scores of colliers tramped their way to and from work along Southwell Lane. Those heroes made up the greatest part of lane activity, men who had known no other working environment for most of their lives, their blackened faces, in the days before pithead baths, labelling their precarious occupation.

For a long time after the Second World War the Summit welcomed men and youths to work there and to keep up its great production. The press carried heavy words of encouragement; 'Come and work in the mines, and know that your working future is assured.'

So the headstock wheels kept turning and the lines carrying trucks away from the coal-loading bays were tremendously busy. Go to the Southwell Lane north end and it was as likely as not you would have to climb over the footbridge to reach Low Moor Road. Activity was that intense.

To the right were the engine sheds, busily dealing with truck trains loaded with precious black diamonds. It was mainly rail transport but there was still the occasional lorry taking its load. The prosperity of coal-turning was an accepted fact, and that fitted in well with the spirit of the times. Hitler was defeated; it was time to look ahead.

There was a verve about in the 1940s, an optimism after all that had been endured. Maybe Vera Lynn marked the time as well as anybody. 'There'll be bluebirds over the White Cliffs of Dover,' the Mistress of Song told us. Sentimental? No doubt, but the country took the song and the singer to its heart. They were truly representative of the period.

The country was getting its breath back and, without a doubt, Kirkby would be proud to be part of the recovery. And what better way to show it than to build for the future, and build was the right word. The planners went to work, and overnight it now seems in retrospect, much of our old lane was cleared. There must have been a bit of heartbreak when the happy band of allotment holders saw what was happening to their beloved gardens. But those in charge of the projected development knew what they had to try to achieve.

House building started and bit by bit – but looking back, with amazing speed – the lane became residential. And, as can well be imagined, there was no shortage of tenants for the new attractive homes. There was obviously consternation when the old outlook disappeared but it was heartening for newlyweds and young families looking for somewhere exciting to live.

And, as if to add variety to the building programme, there was an estate of prefabricated bungalows. 'Ar, somewhere for the old folks,' said more than one local. 'And quite right too,' was the reply of a noted councillor at the time. 'Yes, but will they last?' was a question put forward more than once. 'Just make sure you're around long enough and you'll see,' came the answer. Fifty years later, prefabrication having given way to brick, the old councillor has been proved right. Neat and trim and well cared for, the bungalows are still there. The post-war building blends in splendidly with the lane of the twenty-first century.

As if to add just the right touch, and almost on the edge of the once-visible Speeds' Farm land – and to raise a cheer or two – a public house was built. It was a pub with a surprising name. When the final touches had been made it was christened the Sir Sam. And folk wondered why. Soon they were told: it was named after Sam Orgill, a gentleman of local repute.

But it is no longer the Sir Sam. Tragedy struck, and sadly Sam Orgill died. Fondly remembered even now by some of the older patrons the inn was renamed The Orchid. So the area in that particular part of the lane is remembered for the episode. Now, The Orchid, well patronised, has kept in tune with the changing times and added to the atmosphere of the welcome post-war years.

But suddenly the Summit Colliery ceased production. It was 1968 and the closure meant the loss of over 1,000 jobs despite Lord Robens' statement that 'the potential of the Coal Industry is enormous' when he addressed the NUM Conference in July 1966. Those words were quoted by Mr W.L. Miron, Chairman of the East Midlands Division of the NCB, in a letter he wrote dated 9 September 1966 to reassure a mining employee of continuous employment in coalmining.

So the problems and complexities of a great industry devastated those whose jobs were at the Summit, a colliery sunk in 1883 and closed 85 years later, a mine that had produced a superabundance of coal. Someone stated at the time: 'We were the first pit to raise a million tons, and we kept doing that year after year.' The shutdown of this happy pit came like a bolt from the blue.

And now? No headstock wheels, no loading bays, no footbridge, no engine sheds, no brickyard. And yet, with ingenuity that commercial enterprise always seems to display, much of the old colliery environs have been taken over by firms dealing with, among other things, salvage, building materials, tyres, pattern making, wholesale distribution, fabrics.

Walk down Southwell Lane now and you can't help but admire the way it has become acclimatised to the twenty-first century. Most people it seems have now acquired their own transport, but, as if to make sure, continuous traffic became the order of the day the local planners decided to alter much of the layout of Kirkby's centre. Motorists now save time and temper by using the lane as a cut-through, making it without doubt the busiest secondary road in the district. And, as if to complete the transformation, it is also a bus route, something the old tramping miners would never have believed could possibly happen.

Truly, it is indeed a lane that has turned.

11

Pond Street

I suppose you could pick out almost any street in the Kirkby area and find it bears a few marks with the passing of time. Pond Street would certainly qualify. As a small boy I was told there had been, way back, a pond there. As if it could have received its name for any other reason! But go back in imagination – or in reality if age allows – and what was a hard tamped-down area will have become the focal point of the town. The Wakes have arrived and for a whole week, and occasionally a bit longer, Kirkby will be playing host to the travelling show teams that

Pond Street, 2007. Many of the old-style houses have been replaced with modern bungalows.

Ellis Street, with houses on both sides, was a cut-through to busy Station Street. For a time the main post office was here.

memory says bore well-known names: Proctor, Hibble, Mellor, Cox. Suddenly there is a new dimension: caravans have arrived, all placed in positions that will allow the enormous trailers bringing the razzamatazz of the Wakes to be assembled in the centre space the experienced teams have been accorded.

With ordered hard work and discipline the Pond Hole is transformed in a few short days into the fairground that is part, certainly twice a year, of the Kirkby calendar. On the Thursday maybe, as a sort of tryout for the weekend, a myriad lights are in place, various rides – the prancing horses, the dodgems, the smaller model ponies for the children – are there awaiting eager customers. All a bit sedate in the opening hours, but gradually (and you knew it was going to happen) there is more jostling as the crowd increases, more conviviality as the evening goes on, more investigation of what might be new this time, sorting out where the old attractions and the new have been placed. The clock ticks on, and before you know it, the time has whipped by and you wonder why there is so much you haven't seen. But, you tell yourself, there is always the weekend.

If Thursday was tryout night, by the time Friday got into its stride the Wakes were fully operational and you were just one of scores who knew they had to have a look at the way things were. Maybe to compare the show with what was put on in the autumn visit six months earlier. Certainly there was always eagerness to see if anything new had appeared. But there was always a sharp lookout for the old favourites. And they were there, you could be sure of that.

The thought of those Wakes visits brings back the days of boyhood. Saving one's precious pocket-money for weeks meant that you could 'go to town' on the fairground rides! Sometimes they might be a bit cheaper before six in the evening and such a slice of luck was not to be missed.

Those of a more sophisticated age would cast their eyes – and perhaps their growing expertise – on some of the prizes that might be won by skill on the dartboards; or maybe you might know one of the local boxers who had done his training in the hope of being able to stay three rounds with one of the fairground fighters. Name half-a-dozen of your contemporaries and it was a fair bet they each would have wanted to spend their precious savings on something different from the chums they were with. And Aunt Maud would be prepared to pay her usual Wakes visit to consult the wisdom of palm-reading Gypsy Rose.

But whatever the situation you could be sure that you would be caught up in the raucous good humour of the Wakes no matter who you were with. It was an atmosphere that you couldn't escape whatever your inclinations might be.

But when your pennies had run out it could be a tiring business trying to enjoy the fringe of the excitement. And that was where I was more than a bit lucky. My grandparents lived on Pond Street and at the appropriate time I could slip off and visit them, knowing there would be a cheese sandwich and a glass of homemade lemonade. Very welcome, but the real pull to pay them a call was being able to slip into the parlour, comestibles handy, and peep discreetly from behind the curtain to enjoy so much of the activities by proxy. And sometimes, as a really special treat, Dad and Grandad would let you accompany them to see which local lads were risking their skill in the boxing ring. One or two of them you would know by sight, and there was a sort of kinship because you saw them out and about in the town from time to time, sometimes walking close behind them to enjoy the rub-off of their local reputation as they nodded to acquaintances when they strode up busy Station Street.

And then, much later than your usual supper-time, Grandma would toast you a slice of bread and smooth on to it a generous helping of pork

'*Watch this, boy!*' *A rare shot at a Wakes evening.*

dripping, which you ate as discreetly as you could before Mam said it was time you were off home and to bed.

The walk home was a mile, but you were happy and replete and you knew that if you behaved yourself there was always the possibility of another Wakes evening before the whole charade moved on to another town.

So Pond Street was known to everybody in the growing town. And it was not only because of the Wakes. The residents were mostly well-known established families, mainly of mining stock and happy in their location near the shops at busy weekends.

For a brief time Pond Street had the main post office standing opposite the Co-op Dairy depot and cheek-by-jowl to the Gospel Hall, a place that for a time attracted a growing number of residents, some of whom would be happy to share their new-found faith by singing and Bible-reading in various parts of the town at weekends.

Pastor Jessop, I believe it was, who brought his faith and vigour to the Hall, and for a considerable time the congregation's activities were much in evidence. It was simply another facet of Pond Street that helped swell the considerable bonds of Kirkby's commitment.

Now, just four of the old-type houses remain. At one time there must have been at least twenty of the high solid dwellings. My grandparents lived at no. 21 and years later I was more than a bit amused to see that a new tenant had discarded their number and replaced it with the glorious name of Nirvana, to which a Buddhist or Hindu aspires, explains my dictionary, as the culmination of the meditative state. My Grandma would have chuckled happily, but Grandad would no doubt have been entitled to an explanation as to why a perfectly good number was not acceptable!

Well, no. 21 was later pulled down along with many others. Now, in place of the old houses there are a dozen well-maintained small bungalows neatly placed about the street.

Way back there was always the slight oddity of having practically all the dwellings on one side of the street. Yet it has to be remembered that the sizeable expanse on the south side gave access to the famous Pond Hole.

At one time there was, if not on the street itself, a shop or two in close proximity. Mr Charlesworth's was open for the sale of sweets on the corner of bustling Ellis Street, now no longer packed with houses, but a cut-through never short of traffic. The Co-op butchery was a few strides away from a long-established pawnbroker's managed by Mr Welch. And, close by, on Low Moor Road, Miss Anna Bramley's neat little kiosk offered the very best in confectionery.

And now? Well, no more shops of course, but it was a salutary exercise to make a studied trip (in spite of often using the street) and let time and dreams take over. There is a firm dealing in engineering supplies; a volunteer centre, handy when help is needed; a large and imposing Kirkby Factory Shop; there are also facilities if you need your car valeting.

But dozens of years dissolved as I recalled an occasion when as a schoolboy I went with my father to hear Mr A.J. Cook, a much-respected leader, address a gathering of miners. There were no Wakes on the

Pondhole that night, just scores of miners determined – within reason, for there was much unemployment – to know what the future held for them. The Pondhole had for years been the gathering ground for solidarity.

So what else did my recent Pond Street trip bring back? I remember seeing, when I was very young, the black and silver turnout from the sheds behind the home of Mr Tom Thorpe, a director who brought dignity and splendour to someone's final passing. And I remember standing outside no. 21 and seeing countless passenger and goods trains using the LMS railway at the bottom of the street, with the occasional express hurtling through. I remembered the street corner factory of W. Baines and Co., much in demand as one of the district's foremost building and joinery firms, while on the other corner was an immense banana warehouse.

And finally I remembered my mother, many years after the First World War, unable to keep back loving tears as she told me that her brother always turned at Baines' corner to wave when he went back from leave, before catching his train. But on one particular occasion he didn't wave. It was a moment never forgotten by his family. He returned to his regiment and never made the journey back from the killing fields of France.

12

Remembered Yesterdays

My granddaughter Sarah said to me 'What were your young days really like? What did you do? What games did you play?' I remember the occasion; it must have been a dozen years ago. She had passed her driving test, and that no doubt prompted her remark 'For one thing, there wouldn't have been so many cars about.'

How right she was; and now, London-based, she has some forthright views on traffic problems. But on this day she was keen to know about my boyhood days. I remember holding forth, starting off by recalling the one and only time I saw somebody riding a penny-farthing bicycle.

I was one of a group of children sitting on the pavement on a summer afternoon and, as the rider turned into our street all conversation abruptly stopped. Closing my eyes now I can still see the rider again even at this distance in time. He was a stocky man and had a neat beard. He was wearing a striking green cap and his trousers were held up by braces. He rode along the street (majestically it still seems) to the house close to where we were sitting. I can't recall how he dismounted, but I know he didn't fall off the bike. He simply parked it against some railings and strode up to the house where Mr Wallis lived, one of our neighbours.

Mr Martin's penny-farthing bicycle.

We all examined the cycle but were sitting quietly in our places when the rider (I was told later that he would have been Mr Martin, of Hardy and Martin, mineral-water manufacturers, and for whom Mr Wallis worked) mounted his marvellous machine and pedalled sedately back down the street.

So the penny-farthing episode was just one of four things I remember recalling for Sarah. The others were John Betjeman travelling through

The view John Betjeman would have had passing through Kirkby Bentinck.

Kirkby, following that, naturally enough by stating what a wonderful railway system we had at the time, and then retelling in some detail one of the games the young lads played.

John Betjeman, in his poem 'Great Central Railway – Sheffield Victoria to Banbury', wrote:

> Dark red at Kirkby Bentinck stood
> A steeply gabled farm,
> 'Mid ash trees and a sycamore
> In charismatic calm.

How brilliantly captured, that scene so many of us have known over the years.

Kirkby Bentinck, one of our three railway lines, nestled close to the village of Mayfield, traditionally the home of miners, and way below the fields surrounding the farm. The little station was remembered by so many of us for the Master Cutler, the train that hurtled through from Sheffield to London each workday morning. Nothing should impede this train's timetable, and there had been a few occasions when our morning train, Kirkby Central to Nottingham, had to wait a vital few minutes on the line overlooking Kirkby Quarries for the slightly-delayed Cutler to catch up and make sure it reached London on time. Its schedule was that important.

What railways we had then. Certainly Kirkby must have been one of the best-served towns anywhere in the country. I am prompted to say that when I recall the season tickets I used in my youth. Valid for a month, a ticket could be used for travel between Kirkby and Nottingham. Any of the local stations qualified and travel included weekends. So for 12s 2d – I could use the ticket for thirty-one days. That was certainly value for money.

It wasn't only the cheapness of the railways that made them such an attraction. It was the service. The journey from Kirkby to Nottingham took just 23 minutes on the LNER, and perhaps 5 minutes longer on the Midland because there were more intermediate stations. And, on both lines, there were so many trains to choose from: twenty-four trains up and down from Nottingham each day on the Central line, for example.

The firm I worked for always had a summer outing. It turned out to be Blackpool one year and we made an enquiry of the LNER at Nottingham Victoria. Yes, they could take us on one of their excursions and, provided there were fifty or so in the party, the price would be 4s 6d per head return. Fine, we said, until the LMS got wind of it. Hot-foot their rep came to see us. 'Look,' he said, 'tell me what the LNER are charging.' We told him. 'Right,' he said. 'If they can do it for 4s 6d the LMS will do it for 4s 3d.' That was the measure of the competition in those days. Just how competitive the prices were is shown when one recalls an evening trip from Kirkby to see Matlock illuminations was 2s 6d per head!

One has to bear in mind that, by today's standards, not all that many people managed to get away for a week's holiday, so a trip to the coast was a highlight, and an event like the evening in Matlock was quite an attraction.

Because most of my railway travelling in those days was done on the Kirkby Central line I feel mention has to be made of one of the most remarkable men who worked there. He was Bill Brownhill, officially the station clerk, and the man who signed my season ticket all those years ago. He was a one-armed gentleman. I was told a railway accident had caused his disability.

Although much of his time was spent as a booking clerk it is as a gardener for which he is mainly remembered – by those old enough! It was through his expertise and industry that the tiny station was once a place of delight, colourful summer and winter, deservedly winning prizes in best-kept station competitions. And, as if that were not enough, he was also a great traveller, visiting Spain and Russia in the days when it was unusual for people to travel even as far as Scotland.

Yet that was not all that Bill did. He tended an allotment on railway land opposite the Kirkby police station. He grew vegetables which he sent to Mansfield Hospital. And when it came to Kirkby Carnival Bill appeared in fancy dress as one of the main collectors. A vivid memory is seeing him coming down Chapel Street in loincloth and cotton wrap as Mahatma Gandhi.

The carnival days certainly packed the streets. There was never support lacking when it was needed, and maybe that was because there was room for people to gather, and certainly, I told Sarah, that was the reason we had so many street games handed down over the years.

Dick, Dick, shine a light . . . Tin Lurky . . . Follow my leader . . . But it was Husky-bum, Finger or Thumb that remains so firmly in memory. Not

a game for the faint-hearted or weak-backed. A group of lads – you needed eight or ten – would sort themselves into two groups, and a coin (there was usually somebody who had a ha'penny) would be tossed to see which side would be the jumpers.

The losers would then line up, with the first lad gripping the railings – there had to be a fence – with the second in the team bending down and putting his head between the first lad's legs and holding hard on to his thighs. The third repeated the procedure and so on until the chain was complete. So you had a line of bent backs waiting for the jumpers.

At a given signal the leader of the jumpers would leap as far as he could along the bent backs. Then the next one sprang, and the next, until the whole team were astride. And then? The captain of the jumpers would hold his arm aloft, with the appropriate hand digit extended, and call out: 'Husky-bum, finger or thumb?' There had to be a no-nonsense referee to do the checking and wait for the bent-backed captain's reply. A correct guess and and the teams would swap places; a wrong response and the riding team would line up for another go.

To repeat: not for the nervous!

'I think the girls were right to stick to skipping', said Sarah.

Skipping now, and whipping and topping: they were two activities that always seemed to be in evidence around Shrove Tuesday. And hopscotch for the girls, first carefully chalking the coloured squares on the pavement.

There was never a shortage of activities in the largely empty streets. The occasional delivery van, the very occasional horse and cart, and once in a long while a gentleman on a penny-farthing bicycle. It all went further back than Sarah could remember. 'Yours was a different world', she said. How right she was.

13

Market Eldorado

In its time Kirkby's Market Hall (long since rechristened Festival Hall) was the place to go on Friday evenings if you wanted to pick up a bargain. Secateurs to sealing wax, clothes to cauliflowers, pliers to pomegranates. It was that sort of weekly event and most folk knew what they were looking for. Like many others I found the books on offer were a great attraction whether they were offered for sale on the neatly laid out stall backed up to the high staging and run by a scholarly white-haired gentleman, or a second-hand collection tucked away in the far right-hand

The popular indoor market where the jovial bookseller often stood in the corner.

corner. Money was an important factor and, for me, the new books were mainly tied in with birthdays and Christmases.

The seller of the second-hand books was a jovial soul with a taste for colourful jackets and bow-ties, an effect that seemed to brighten his wares. His stall had scores of books neatly presented row upon row, packed as tight as rush-hour travellers, and there were a couple of small side tables loaded to their creaking capacity, no arranging of authors or titles; over everything a glorious disarray.

What Katy Did lay side by side with some blazing Western, and a much-thumbed hymnal kept company with a treatise on beekeeping. As widely varied as the titles were the people who probed among them. The little old lady peering through her glasses jostled the burly man whose inspection had an air of abandon, a contributor to scuffed backs and ruffled pages. The schoolgirl squinted along the same row as the connoisseur.

Sometimes it was possible to pick up a real treasure. That I know, for I once paid a humble shilling for Boswell's *Life of Johnson*, published in 1830. For such bargains your collector will browse for hours, and if good fortune comes his way he will accept it gratefully, feeling he has stolen a march on other hunters.

The busy corner had many fascinations, and not least were the fragments scribbled on the fly-leaves of some of the books. They were like roughly-cut diamonds; the polish and setting were left to the imagination. 'May our friendship ripen – John.' Was the book sent after a dinner in some old inn, with fairy lights hanging from the beams? Did the wine make John's blood race and lead him to hope? There were those and a dozen other questions. But there was an inevitable one. Why was a book with such an inscription lying there marked '6d to clear'?

There was another. 'Carry this if you care – Emily.' Could anything be more intriguing? Emily had not prefaced the inscription with a name, but we can be sure it was aimed at some male heart. Was Emily spurned then, for this slim volume of poetry to reach the corner table? But wait a moment. There was a sonnet, two lines of which were underscored.

> And in the pale and silver'd morn
> Her feet so gently tread the dew.

At the bottom of the page there was a terse note which told all. 'This might be Emily herself.' George, or Richard, had evidently cared.

I felt more than once that the Kirkby Friday Market's little corner was a haven where a man, or woman, could cheat the world, even to the weather.

At the appropriate time the old building was renamed Festival Hall.

When the snowflakes danced in the sky you could reach out and go to sunny Spain. While the wind roared, and the rain swirled against the window behind the jovial bookman, you could share the warmth of some character or other of the calibre of Mr Pickwick. Or you could stand against the cool wall on a boiling July day and go south with Scott.

More than one local worker must have left desk or shop at the end of a gruelling day and, after a brief spell in the book corner, sauntered home to an evening's rest in the company of memorable characters who live in a treasured book enlivened by the jovial gent who once added quite a bit to Kirkby's Friday market.

14

Two Remembered Heads

It must be nearly sixty years since I saw Miss Lilian Quinion stride into St Wilfrid's for Sunday morning service. I handed her a prayer-book and she went into her customary pew. A smiling and still fresh-faced lady of slightly less than average height.

Twenty years before that time she had been, for three years, someone I saw, apart from school holidays, five days a week. I can't say I recollect the first time she came into my life, but it couldn't have been long after the initial sighting that I became well aware of her presence.

Miss Quinion was the headmistress of what the locals called 'the little school'. 'Little' was used simply because it was the junior school

A recent photograph of the 'little school', now converted to a private residence.

Miss Sharman, left, and Miss Quinion, right, with forty serious-looking youngsters photographed in the 1920s.

in our part of Kirkby. Church Street Infants, as it was officially known, was by the standards of the day perhaps a bit on the small side. There always seemed to be plenty of infants hurtling about the place at playtimes.

Once you had became one of the school's pupils you would have noticed Miss Quinion's high colour under her permanent straw hat. And she always seemed to wear a long knitted cardigan wrapped close to her figure, entirely in keeping with her plaid skirt and thick brown shoes. If all the school's teachers had been assembled you would have had little difficulty in identifying her as the headmistress.

She was simply a formidable lady, and of that I was aware quite soon after I saw her. You knew, even though you were only five years old, that she was someone who had her schoolchildren under control. The other teachers on the staff were certainly no pushovers but, looking back, Miss Quinion had an air that set her apart.

It was maybe a couple of years after starting at the school that she said to me: 'I want you to take this small parcel to the Co-op shop just down the street. Tell someone who works behind the counter that it is from Miss Quinion. There is no answer, so when you have handed it over come back here. And don't run. I don't want you to be falling over. Is that clear?'

'Yes, Miss Quinion,' I said, and went towards the schoolyard gate with what I hoped was acceptable decorum. Don't run? Well, she didn't say you couldn't hop or skip a bit, so I tried both simple means of locomotion simply because it was so marvellous to be outside the school perimeter even though the shop was barely a hundred yards away. So this was the world occupied by the adults when their children were at school? Terrific. If I behaved myself I might, who knows, get the chance to run another errand. But I bet she timed me, and never again was I sent to join the world outside the school walls.

But there was a day when I did cause a bit of consternation. Like all the other kids I was running about helter-skelter in the playground when I took a real tumble, gashed my knee, and was frightened because I knew my mother would be most unhappy if the blood got on to my clothes. Someone told Miss Sharman. She came over in a hurry, did very little fussing, and miraculously produced a cloth which she used to tidy me up. Gently she brought me to a sitting position, fetched a canvas chair and, with the help of another teacher whose name I have forgotten, took me inside the school and stretched me out on a rug in front of the fire in the big hall.

Then Miss Quinion appeared. There were a few words exchanged by the ladies. Miss Sharman went off for further schoolyard supervision, and the headmistress, now minus her hat over silver hair, fetched a medical box, returned quickly, and went to work. 'Now boy,' she said, 'I must attend to you. It's a nasty gash you've got but I am sure you will be all right.' She put a bandage over the injury, told me to be quiet for the rest of the morning, and walk home carefully at lunchtime. 'I shall give you a note to take to your mother,' she said. And then, wonder of wonders, she smiled and patted my head. It was almost worth falling over to be accorded that gesture.

I limped when I went home but my mother was not deceived. She told me that if I was careful I would be all right to get off back to school in the afternoon. 'And it was very good of Miss Quinion to write a note to me,' she said.

But to be patted on the head by Miss Q! That was enough to give any pupil at Church Street School new strength to face the world. It didn't however stop me being very wary of the headmistress. She had a school to run, and she ran it, beneath that distinctive straw hat and in that long woollen cardigan. I would dearly have loved to ask her if she had retained her hat as a souvenir when I saw her those many years later as she strode up for Morning Prayer at St Wilfrid's. But it was so heartening to see her, now smiling and wonderfully friendly, that there were other topics of conversation.

There was however, one incident about which I would have liked to remind her. It was the time when the Parliamentary Elections were held during my time at her school. A large poster, red lettering on a white background, was stuck on one of the large gates on the side of the playground facing Church Street.

Mr F. Seymour Cocks was the Labour candidate for Broxtowe, which in those long gone days covered Kirkby. The poster was put up just before the election and I remember very well being one of countless little lads running home at lunchtime and shouting 'Vote for Labour and Seymour Cocks!' Well, that was what it said on the poster. So what was all the fuss about when I dashed into our home, still shouting the instruction, to see my mother suddenly lift up her apron to cover her face – as she often did when she was embarrassed – and then reappear to show tears of laughter running down her cheeks? With difficulty she composed herself and managed to blurt out: 'Come on now! Forget that for a bit, pull up your chair and eat your rice pudding.'

Would Miss Quinion have smiled if I'd reminded her? I like to think she would.

She lived for many years on Sutton Road – the house is still there – with her lady companion; and when the day came that they left Kirkby to live the rest of their days in Budleigh Salterton I certainly wouldn't be the only one whose early years were guided by her, and who quietly wished her well.

I left Church Street Infants to go to Chapel Street School. Like all the others who made the switch at the same time I was eight years old. We had said our mumbled goodbyes to the red-faced and sometimes severe Miss Quinion, and were received into the new school by a massive largely bald man who had the habit of scrutinising you from his considerable height.

He was John George Davison. He smiled a lot, was obviously on good terms with his staff and, as the occasion offered itself, very much at ease with his pupils. Without making a habit of it he had been known to join in their playground games; he could do a tricky dribble or two with a tennis ball and, if someone had made a slide (but it always had to be against the wall) it was not unknown for him to take his turn to do a bit of sliding, his large lemon-coloured brogue shoes very much in evidence. 'Come on, keep on the move,' he would order in severe winter weather.

He didn't have an office so far as I can remember, but he did have a large desk at the end of the school hall. Behind that desk, always seemingly busy, he spent a good deal of his working day. But he never neglected going around the school, visiting each class in turn. When we left Church Street for Chapel Street we had three long years in front of us to get some knowledge into our heads. There was a talented staff – Miss Kirk, Miss Dickinson, Miss Lindley, Miss Machin, Mr Allcock, Mr Reeve and, for a short time, Irish Molly, large, forbidding, sometimes quite humorous, a lady of quite considerable proportions.

So John George Davison was a busy man most of the time and seemed to make his rounds without getting put out. He must have had his problems of course because there were one or two difficult boys. There seemed to be an understood method for dealing with those who stepped out of line. Most of the teachers had been in the profession for a considerable time and knew the tactics necessary to keep the peace. If there was some deviation it was then the teacher could be driven to say: 'Right, another episode like that and you will be seeing Mr Davison.' That was usually sufficient deterrent.

If the threat had to be carried out, once was usually enough. It meant going into the hall where the great man would more than likely be sitting behind his large desk, knowing, you might be sure, that someone was there. But he chose not to look up until he thought it appropriate. That in itself was punishment enough. When he did look up, followed by standing up, you felt you were facing a colossus.

And when he said: 'Right, you will stay in today at playtime.' Well, that was bad enough, but it was what came next that was more unsettling. You waited for it. He had one or two sentences but the usual one was 'Today I have been wasting my time in class and that will not do.' He then fished in his drawer and came out with a large sheet of paper. 'You will write that sentence twenty-five times, and I want it writing as well as you can.' He would then pause, look at the offender and say: 'Is that clear?'

'Yes sir,' you said in your best desk-side manner.

But all was not quite finished. The head then said, more than likely: 'And if your writing isn't as good as I think it should be you'll have to give up your playtime until it is. Understand?'

'Yes sir,' you said again, and then you were told to go. Thinking about that now it seems a trivial punishment, but it wasn't; it meant you would be missing one or more playtimes, that break when you were free to hare about with your pals. That was the punishment.

But the great thing with JGD was that the next day, if the opportunity presented itself and he felt inclined, he would have a spell of catching a ball with a selected group. And you could be sure he would at an appropriate assembly in the hall come out with his much-admired verse:

> If you run you may win the race:
> Should you lose 'twill be no disgrace.
> You run!

The final two words were delivered in a tremendous voice with his arms flung wide to give additional emphasis. Mr Davison was a rounded personality, someone who seemingly didn't bear grudges, but made the best of each day, in school or out of it.

He must have been one of the first caravanners in the area. He kept his mobile home in the field at the top of the railway embankment on Southwell Lane, where he could keep an eye on it. He brought it out whenever there was the chance to take a few days in his beloved Scarborough. His wife, with her youthful spirit, seemed to complement him. Their children, Derek and Veronica, were given no favours at school and were very happy to mix with the rest of us during their time there.

JGD was known by scores of parents who had children at Chapel Street School as Daddy Davison. I can remember, when I was panicking because I couldn't find a simple bit of homework, that my mother, who eventually found the piece of paper I needed, saying: 'Here, and take good care of it or we shall have Daddy Davison coming to see us.'

He had been quite an athlete in his time, so my father told me, and once when Dad and I, many years later, had gone on to the immense sweep of ground we all called the Cowpastures to see the start of a cross-country race, the old head stood beside us. 'What a wonderful spectacle this is to be sure. Such colours, and what endeavour there will have to be to win a race of this sort.'

J.G. Davison, friendly yet formidable.

'Could you have managed it once?' my Dad asked.

'I might have enjoyed trying,' said Daddy Davison, 'if I'd been forty years younger and half my weight, and with a bit of thatch to take the sweat.'

When the old headmaster died his vigorous wife continued to live in the house they had shared for many years, darting about Kirkby with a rucksack on her back. But the time came when she too died and eventually the house was put up for sale. But not before the considerable library had been offered to the public. A great day that, but a sad one. Their reading had been wide, saying much about two extraordinary people.

15

When the Pictures
Started Talking

Kirkby, like many other places in Britain, went through an exciting
time around three-quarters of a century ago. The taIkies came to
town. It was a shot in the arm for the entertainment industry and
there was the promise of great times ahead. The Star and the
Kings were established cinemas and great things were expected from the
imposing building being erected at the centre of the town. That was to be
the Regent, and such was its anticipated splendour perhaps that is where
we should start.

My first memory of the Regent was seeing large pink title letters flashed
up quite suddenly as I walked with my parents along Low Moor Road in
1930. It was on 6 October that the much-lauded cinema took in its first
customers. This was it then, the talkies had arrived. There had been silent
films here and there – sometimes special shows in various public halls – but
this we were told was the dawn of a new age.

Mansfield had been lucky enough to have a talkie cinema for some time
and I well remember hearing a neighbour saying, a touch of wonder in her
voice: 'It's true what they say. You can hear as well as see. I mean, we went
last week and there was this cow on the screen. I nearly jumped out of my
seat when it mooed. True, you could hear it!' She'd certainly been
impressed, having been a picture fan for a long time and making the trip to
Mansfield most weeks. Her world, she admitted, had moved into a new
dimension. It was obviously the moo that did it!

The newspapers (and particularly *The Picturegoer*) had told us what
we could expect in the new age that had dawned here and in America,
and which was now going to be brought to our little town to entertain and
educate us.

'Well, that's it then. Books are finished,' pronounced one of my elderly
relatives. 'I mean, who's going to sit reading when you can toddle off to the
pictures and get it all done for you while you're in an armchair enjoying

A cinema with a colourful past.

every minute of it without wondering what the author's babbling on about?'

Maybe it did make a difference to the book trade, but not adversely. I well remember how Sapper's publicity increased when his *Bulldog Drummond* appeared on the screen. And Edgar Wallace, with Gordon Harker the ideal man to act in his Cockney stories, certainly wouldn't have been complaining.

The first film at the Regent was *The Desert Song*, with John Bowles' rich voice filling the cinema with dialogue and song. 'Well, it'll kill the theatre,' my relative said, determined to prove his point.

But he was wrong again. The theatre still flourished, and drew full houses, especially when a film star was appearing – Jessie Matthews for instance – at Nottingham's Theatre Royal. We were, in fact, living in a new world, and for many locals a weekly trip to the Regent was something not to be missed.

It comes back so easily the long list of films that came in those faraway days. *Rio Rita* followed *The Desert Song*. Although the titles get a bit mixed up on recall the actors and actresses are all stored in memory. Wheeler and Wolsey, Charlie Chaplain, Tom Mix and the cowpunchers who were so popular. Want a few? Well there was Hoot Gibson, Ken Maynard, Buck Jones, Tim McCoy, all able to deal with anybody trying to alter the layout of the Wild West. No wonder we lads all boasted owning six-shooters, some of which were capable of making a bang on the paper caps against which you could pull your trigger.

And the comedy stars: Harold Lloyd, Buster Keaton, Ben Turpin; larger than life figures whose antics could make quite a difference to your weekend. The girls were not outdone of course. They could dote over the romantic roles played by Greta Garbo, Marlene Dietrich, Laura la Planta and Gracie Fields. No doubt the screen heroines had an effect on them, just as the lads were able to adopt a swagger for a day or two imitating their celluloid heroes.

A new world for the children and certainly a new world for the adults. Friday and Saturday evenings were so popular that if there was some film showing at the Regent that had received good notices it likely as not meant seats had to be booked (usually in the 'one-and-nines') so that they could turn up knowing accommodation was waiting. Take a chance and that could mean joining a queue tightly packed for 50yds or so up Diamond Avenue.

Occasionally a much-acclaimed film would be showing all week (Monday to Saturday) but more often the programme, such was the popularity of the new medium, would be changed mid-week, a boon to those who had the time and the money to watch what was on twice a week. Something special – Robert Donat for instance in *The Ghost Goes West*, or Robert Newton in *Treasure Island* – would ensure a packed house whenever it was showing.

So much for the Regent with its friendly staff under the keen eye of manager Mr Whitfield. And, we mustn't forget, although there was no chance of a film being shown on a Sunday in those early days, just occasionally there would be a concert given by one of the local brass bands. So accomplished were the day's instrumentalists that a full house could be guaranteed, but only after the churches and chapels were emptied of their congregations.

Kirkby in those days was lucky. There was, in addition to the Regent, a refurbished Kings and a modernised Star. The Kings, built in 1912, was perhaps the smallest of Kirkby's cinemas but it had its share of locals who kept a sharp eye for its films, and maybe there was a real attraction in

The Kings cinema was eventually demolished.

that it was situated only a few yards away from the ancient Railway Inn. That is not to say the cinema's customers were a bit wobbly before they took their seats in the auditorium, but it was a handy meeting place for a nightcap and a discussion on the merits of the evening's entertainment.

A small balcony was added to the cinema in 1919 which gave a cosy atmosphere to the place. On the ground floor there was an arrangement with the cheapest seats called 'the chicken run' occupying a marked area nearest the screen. The chicken run was certainly the right place to be when there was the added attraction of a live act on the programme. The Kings was never short of good screen entertainment and at first the live act arrangement happened only infrequently, but it was often enough to make sure the seats were filled. One act in particular is still remembered. Saxon Brown, billed as the World's Strongest Man, made an appearance in 1932.

When Saxon's act was announced (the curtains had been drawn across the stage) there was absolute silence. A longish wait and the curtains slowly parted to reveal the strongman clad in dressing gown and flanked by a heavyweight gentleman on either side. Slowly Saxon took off his gown and even from the back row of the chicken run he looked a massive figure. One

A rare photograph of the Star displaying a poster for a Western – The Bushranger, *a film from 1928.*

of his assistants was holding a rope. We waited a few more moments and watched spellbound as the rope was put round Saxon's neck and each end held by one of the assistants. Suddenly they started to pull against the rope which was held by the strong man either side of the loop round his neck.

How long did the men pull? Certainly long enough for the spectators to maintain an entranced silence, but suddenly the rope went slack as the two men crumpled under the strain of their endeavours. Saxon Brown, legs slightly apart, stood as steady as a rock; serenely he let the rope fall and stood back to take the plaudits of the audience.

But all was not over. The strongman proceeded to carefully lie down on a slightly raised nailed platform that had been brought on to the stage. A stout board was then given to him and he held it on his chest. The two rope men were each given a long-handled heavy hammer and at a given signal they pounded away in turn on the board. For some electrifying minutes the hammering was the only sound in the cinema. Then suddenly the pounding ceased and the hammerers helped Saxon off his bed of nails to tumultuous applause.

Was there some trick involved? Very soon we would know. The unbelievable strongman, still steady on his feet, left the stage and walked

Saxon Brown pulling a Midland General bus – with his teeth!

down into the auditorium. I can remember so well sitting in one of the end seats. His back bore many nail marks but there were no punctures to the skin. Strangely the applause had given way to silence as the great man did his walkabout, but when he climbed back on to the stage the Kings erupted. Those present had obviously witnessed a miracle. Seventy-five years later I can still marvel at the recollection of the occasion.

One thing is for sure: I don't remember what picture was showing. Nor, I suppose, does any other now-ancient lady or gent who happened to be there. After what we had witnessed, celluloid figures on a screen were not very important.

Saxon Brown obviously believed in giving value for money, and to make sure Kirkby remembered his visit to the Kings he provided an outstanding feat of strength on the road just in front of the cinema on the Saturday morning of his week-long appearance.

A rope was attached to a Midland General bus and Saxon pulled it. He actually pulled it. Must have had strong arms did you say? Oh certainly, he had strong arms, but he didn't use them for this incredible demonstration. He pulled the bus with his teeth! And there is a photograph to prove it.

Now the Kings management couldn't be expected to bring such stage acts every week, but that didn't stop them adding to whatever was billed in the world of cinema. And if variety is the spice of entertainment then variety is what the Kings customers were offered.

In its later years, when Mr Alf Wall took over as manager, he encouraged many local people to show their talents. Surprisingly there was a good supply – singers, comedians, and even a star yodeller. He also broke new ground by inviting local amateur societies to put on one-act plays. He was nothing if not enterprising and the public responded.

The films kept pace; there was never a shortage of up-to-date releases to bring in the enthusiasts but eventually the cinema – and one can only assume the advent of television played no minor part in it – closed in the early 1960s.

Since then there have been various enterprises on the site – it was once a petrol station and car showroom – and now, the building still solid and trim, shows an attractive front to the world of commerce.

Sadly, the Railway Inn, a near neighbour well before and after the lifetime of the Kings, has recently been demolished, taking with it a bit of history from the days when the town had a population of little more than seven thousand.

There has been much worth recording in Kirkby's recent history but not many episodes more entertaining than the week when Saxon Brown was a visiting phenomenon.

The Star was for years an attractive cinema on Kingsway. It was managed impeccably by Mr Percy Thorpe who was served by a very courteous staff. Neatly arranged all on one level it had its share of the latest films although on one well remembered occasion – when I was one of many waiting to be admitted – Mr Thorpe came out to tell us that the film for the evening had not arrived. 'But I am assured it will he here very shortly. If you would like to wait inside there is an ice cream for you with the compliments of the management.'

Well, that was not a bad deal I suppose, and it was made even better when, shortly after the ice cream had been eaten, the film did arrive, we took our chosen seats and the evening's entertainment began.

Mr Thorpe, experienced in the ways of the cinema trade, took it all in his stride and the audience, now considerably increased, spent an hilarious hour in the company of Will Hay and his scholars.

The Star always seemed a less rumbustious place than the other two Kirkby cinemas, although that may be because I only seemed to be there when there was a film I particularly wanted to see.

One film I certainly had no intention of missing was *Excuse My Glove*, featuring my schoolboy hero Len Harvey who was recognised by the British Boxing Board of Control as the Light Heavyweight Champion of the World. I wrote to the great man and he responded by sending me an autographed photo of himself.

One of the things I remember about the Star is the wall decorations.

They were stylish but very unusual and when you sat waiting for the lights to go down you could have kidded yourself that you were in the world of the pharaohs. Without doubt they were strange and quite distinctive and I always felt there was a strong Egyptian influence. That was it; you felt there was more than a touch of the pyramids.

The Star had its stage activities too. For a time there was a strong musical tradition in the Kirkby district and many of the stage turns put on were well within the demand of fifty or sixty years ago, including one or two solo performers, violinists and piano-accordion players, and on the odd occasion there would be choirs giving well-applauded renderings.

One particular evening comes to mind when a local church choir did a concert devoted to the tunes of the First World War, with the chance of the audience to join in for 'Pack Up Your Troubles' and 'It's A Long Way to Tipperary'.

On one occasion there was a departure from what one had come to expect. A large glass tank filled with water was on the stage when the curtains parted, into which a well-stripped gentleman stepped. The exhibitionist, with assistants ready in case of need, remained completely immersed for what seemed a very long time before he steadily resurfaced, having lain in the tank without any breathing apparatus. This drew much applause, but it was certainly an event I had no wish to see repeated.

The Star closed its doors as a cinema for the last time on 28 September 1957. Its final film, appropriately enough, was *Showdown at Abilene*. The premises, employed over time by various companies, now form part of much-used Kingsway.

The Regent? It had a truly entertaining past, and now, after various commendable efforts, one hopes it will eventually have a future its position merits.

16

Two in Their Time

It seems to me that the days of my boyhood were memorable chiefly on account of people having time. Having time to walk, to talk, to lean over garden gates, to sit and look around. Even in our busily growing little town there was space. There can be little doubt, of course, that boyhood added to this sense of space, but green fields and quiet roads there were and, even allowing for the mists of memory to play their part, people moved a deal slower before the combustion engine became such a confounded necessary nuisance.

And if my boyhood had this sense of spaciousness, how much more it must have been when my grandfather was young.

Joe was my maternal grandfather, and my first memory of him is seeing him towering over me as I sat on the red-and-white patterned sofa in the living room at Pond Street. I have been keen on boxing for as long as I can remember and Joe must be partly responsible for this. He said something to me and I slipped off the sofa and put my fists up to him. His blue eyes twinkled and his snow-white moustache stood out sharply against his ruddy cheeks.

'Why, I'll drop thi' one on thi' weskit button,' he said, and made as if to do just that. Whether he did or not I can't recall, but it was the only time I ever squared up to him. At about four years of age there didn't seem a great deal of risk. There would have been a tremendous risk as I grew older.

Even while I was a small boy I had the feeling when I was with him that he was simply a gentle tiger, and that gentleness was always self-imposed. He was literally afraid of no man – a tough, uncompromising character. The times I saw him lose his temper were few and far between, but when he did he seemed to me as mighty as Hercules.

There were times when I had him eating out of my hand. My parents encouraged me to learn bits of poetry so that I would be able to

Grandma and Grandad's long-serving Pond Street gramophone.

Grandma and Grandad outside their Orchard Road home.

recite when we paid our weekend visit to Pond Street. I had to stand on the tiny stool on which Joe liked to rest his feet. Joe and my grandmother loved it, and so did I. There's little doubt about it, when kids have to perform it is really showing off for the sake of the parents. Not that I blame my mother and father. Certainly, in my young days they had little enough brightness in their lives – what with working conditions and the rest – so maybe I helped a bit. We moan nowadays – 'all part of the business of living I suppose' – but the early part of the twentieth century must have been desperately hard.

They were the days of large families. Joe and Ann had eight children. Six survived beyond childhood; two died very young. Which meant years of childbearing for my grandmother. And in what conditions? Aunt Mary spoke of the house as being big enough for the whole family. There were two full-size bedrooms and a small one. Even accounting for some disparity in the ages of the children there must nearly always have been seven or eight about the place. Maybe sleeping wasn't so much of a problem then: it wasn't unusual to have three in a bed.

But there was no bath, there was hot water from the fireplace boiler only, the rooms were small, the windows were small, there was gas lighting in the downstairs rooms, and no lighting at all in the bedrooms. There may have been a carpet in the front room but that is doubtful; mainly the floors were red quarry bricks covered by an assortment of rugs. There was a sofa in the living room to give the only bit of real comfort; the rest of the seating was hard chairs. True, there were armchairs in the front room, as well as a sofa, but the front room was used only on highdays and holidays so that didn't count.

The toilet was one of about four standing in a row across the backyard. As long as I can remember it was a flush model, but that must have been something out of the ordinary, for in our district the conversion of toilets from earth to flush did not take place until about 1928. With a large family it must have been something of a procession backwards and forwards across the yard. Small wonder that one of my abiding memories is of my grandmother lifting the living-room curtain and smiling down at me as I watered the grate under the scullery window.

My grandmother originated from the village of Brailes in Warwickshire. She had followed her farmhand brother to find work in Pinxton, where she fell in love with and married miner Joe Jordan who was twice her size. She seemed to dress mainly in dark clothes, which set off her ruddy complexion. She had small, sharp eyes, and she laughed a lot. She certainly seemed to find something to laugh at in most of my remarks. I can close my eyes and hear her saying: 'Well did you now?' or 'Now that's one I shall have to tell your Grandad.' Her voice was high and squeaky but she never seemed to carry on a conversation; her remarks were mainly confined to a sentence or two. Because I knew it pleased Joe I would kiss her on her forehead now and then – even as a little lad I could quite easily manage that – and it always seemed to please her.

Joe was a feared bare-knuckle fighter in the Kirkby district. I never heard him talk about his fights but I heard of his reputation from a good many who had known him. 'He was never very scientific,' said my father, 'but he was as hard as a brick. He could take punishment and he could dish it out.' As I remember him I can imagine this would be so. He would stand foursquare and it would be like trying to uproot a tree.

One fight I heard most about was against a man called Crabby Ward. Crabby was reckoned to be 'cock of the midden' around Kirkby. Insults of one sort or another had been bandied about, and Joe had sprung to the side of a friend, so the story went. The fight was fixed for a Sunday afternoon on Hogg's Lane, half-way up Diamond Avenue. My father, then a lad at school, was one of the spectators. The betting was heavily in Crabby's favour.

Father was a bit hazy about how long the fight lasted, but said: 'They were going at it for the best part of an hour. Crabby could make no impression on Joe and he certainly didn't get the better of him.' 'Who won?' I asked. 'I don't think either of 'em won,' Dad replied. 'It was stalemate. But one thing I can tell you: Crabby Ward never wanted to fight Joe again. He knew he'd met his match.'

I don't think for one moment my father was spoofing when he said that. I remember one man whose opinion I always valued, and who was not given to exaggeration, saying 'Joe could hold his own wi' the best of 'em.'

Harry Peach, Joe's neighbour for a number of years, and a lifelong friend, could recount a tale or two. Harry thought very highly of Joe's prowess, and he could speak from first-hand experience, for their friendship had remained firm through good times and bad. Said Harry, with a wistful look in his old eyes: 'For my money it were Joseph every time.'

In Joe's heyday there was a good deal of cockfighting too, and my father told of a trip being made into Staffordshire in support of a local bird. There would have been a deal of betting. Joe had done his share of betting and at one period didn't seem to be short of cash. It seems his occasional gambling exploits had helped swell his bank balance.

In many ways they were cruel days. True, there was some fun amid the gloom, but it was only a tiny percentage of what humans had a right to expect, and which, in these enlightened days they would demand. But the rank and file workers then looked upon very little as being their rights.

But through the darkness chinks of light were appearing. My father told of walking (and Joe was among the walkers) from Kirkby to Bulwell Common to hear A.J. Cook, the miners' leader, speak. True, they were spacious days, and when you walked to Bulwell you knew that. It was 10 miles there and 10 miles back home!

Joe was by no means an agitator. He was essentially a worker, a man who could hold his own with the best man they could put beside him. But he knew his rights and he recognised the rights of others. Like practically all the miners in the Kirkby area he wouldn't have dreamt of missing a political meeting. The miners were groping towards the light, but they were still under the protective wings of the coal-owners.

Without men like Joe there would have been no coal-owners, but there was great need for leadership allied to organisation, allied to funds. The smouldering unrest was there, but there was little danger of fire because miners needed to work to keep body and soul together, to feed the all-too-often hungry mouths of their wives and children. But the movement was moving inch by inch towards a better day. The miners were moulding their case, learning how to present themselves. They were stumbling towards a new dawn. Joe didn't live long enough to see the full sunrise, but he did see the dawn break. His great heart beat with the hearts of his fellow toilers, and meantime he slogged it at the coal-face.

One thing was for certain: Grandma expected her housekeeping money. More than once I saw her hold out her apron for the coins and odd note or two to be dropped in it. 'I've got to watch him,' I'd heard her say, and she'd turned to whoever was there and give an exaggerated wink. But there was never any question of Grandad trying on any deceit. 'And that's for you m'dear,' I'd heard him say as he stooped to kiss her.

Some years before his retirement, due to strikes and mining unrest, Joe sought other work. He had a spell when he was employed as part of a team laying tar on the Kirkby roads, and then he became a gravedigger for the local council. And of course he had a tale or two to tell; one in particular was the occasion when he had to reopen a grave for a second interment and his foot went through the coffin lid holding the body inside.

I can recall him saying on one occasion 'They'll need a lot more than me doing this job if Hitler has his way.' And when war broke out he was saddened. 'This'll do nobody any good,' he predicted. I often recalled his words and thought a good deal about him and Grandma while I was in the forces: it was a sad day when I had a letter from my mother to tell me that the old lady had died.

And I recalled too the occasion when he once said to me: 'Ten bob apiece ain't a deal for me and your Grandma to get fat on.' How right he was: it certainly underlined the prevailing conditions. The pension they received from the government for the son they'd lost in Flanders in the First World War obviously helped eke things out a bit, and went towards the cost of the house they bought when they left Pond Street for Orchard Road. But the move had an unsettling effect on Grandma and they finished up in a council bungalow in the Homesteads where, with a living room and one bedroom they could more easily cope.

When Joe was left to live on his own my mother worked like a Trojan for him. She was the relative who lived nearest and he expected daily attendance, particularly the delivery of his midday meal. He had never been demonstrative but he could become exasperating if there was a break in the routine. He had lived for more than eighty years and it was too much to expect him to alter his ways. A good meal at twelve o'clock sharp did much to harmonise his day.

Personal cleanliness was a lifelong habit, and every day while he was able he would strip to the waist and give himself a thorough dowsing. 'Get stripped to the buff, lad. You can't beat it.' Fitness was a great thing with him and washing well and often was part of his creed. And when he was stripped, what a man! Even in his last years he looked like a great oak, and you saw at once why there were few men willing to dispute his word.

The other thing that had to be on time was delivery of his evening paper, particularly in the cricket season. I had never heard of him playing but he was a great lover of the game; there was nothing he enjoyed more in his younger days than spending a day at Trent Bridge with my father. Given the slightest opportunity he would recall some episode he had witnessed at the county ground. He would close his eyes in memorable relish. 'I remember seeing George Gunn', he would say, 'batting against Tich Freeman. My word, it were brains against brains were that.'

He never missed the Whitsuntide match at Trent Bridge for years, and could reel off the Nottinghamshire and Surrey teams spanning more than one decade. It was a trick of his to name a cricketer, close his eyes, and then, slowly – eyes still closed – wag his head, as though to say: 'We'll never see another like him.' 'Jack Hobbs,' he would say, and then go into his eye-closing ritual. 'Andy Ducat'; 'Ranji': 'C.B. Fry.'

But his favourites were Joe Hardstaff (Old Joe he used to call him, to distinguish between him and his famous son) and Topsy Wass. 'Owd Topsy,' he would say, and regale you with a description of the man, his run-up, the fiery ball hurled at the nervous batsman, and then refer to his questionable language. But his love for Joe Hardstaff senior carried over on Old Joe's retirement to Young Joe, and one of the last questions he asked me was how many runs Young Joe had scored the previous day. The match, strangely enough, was against Surrey. 'Thirty-five not out at close of play' I said. 'Ah, that's not bad for a start,' he murmured, propped up on his deathbed.

17

Remembering Chapel Street & the Long Whit Walks

It was an interesting experience to find myself after a considerable time in the function room of the Waggon and Horses, one of the old and popular hostelries in Kirkby. Immediately I was reminded of the time when I had been invited to watch Oliver Stafford (Kid Staff) in training for the vacant area welterweight championship. He looked superbly fit and it was at one time thought he would make the highest grade in the fight game.

For various reasons Oliver didn't carry on as long as most local enthusiasts thought he should have done, but he certainly did his bit to put on some sterling shows at the old Market Hall.

Those were the days when, if you were keen enough – and I was – you got out of bed in the middle of the night to listen to broadcasts crackle their way across the Atlantic, and strained to hear the voices of Raymond Glendenning or Stewart McPherson (with inter-round summaries by W. Barrington Dalby of course) as Tommy Farr fought Jim Braddock and then, on another occasion, Joe Louis.

But, to stay in Kirkby, that was the time when there were fortnightly boxing shows put on at the Market Hall, and for 5s you could get a ringside seat. So, being in the Waggon, as it is affectionately known throughout the district, was a time for recollections of boxing and many other things beside.

Across from the pub was a stone cottage then known as Brailsford's Corner. It had been for many years the home of Arthur Brailsford, leading light of the Kirkby Saddle Club. He was not only a keen horseman, but for a long time had been headmaster of Selston School. But he always spent as much time as he could with the horses he stabled in the commodious yard.

It was an interesting place hereabouts. The house on the other side of the pub car park was a distinctive ivy-covered building. When I was young it was the home of Mr Hancock, a dentist who had his practice in Sutton. But the important part of his departure as he set off for work each morning – for us lads anyway – was not whether he was late, but the super car he drove off in. It was a Frazer-Nash, grey and large by the standards of the day, with a leather strap over the bonnet in the best racing-car tradition. And he was always seen off by his wire-haired fox terrier who had taken up its privileged position on top of the stone wall that bounded the garden.

On the same side as the Hancock house, a few yards further down, was Broom House, a stone cottage (long gone) that was occupied for many years by the Misses Fox, one of whom was a noted herbalist.

Some of the lads who were around at the time had good reason to be wary of the herbalist. Not for her potions but because, when she and her sister moved to live on Park Street, the back garden of their house bordered the piece of land we all called Kirkby Park, and on which we played football in winter and cricket in summer. Inevitably, it was not unknown for a ball from either game to land among their cabbages. Or could it have descended on some obscure herb that was being grown for the herbalist's patients?

On one occasion she reported us to the police, and the consequence was that a notice was nailed to one of two very large trees forbidding the playing of ball games. That was too much for one or two of us, and under cover of darkness we managed to remove the notice and lay it in a patch of long grass. But the herbalist was too cunning for us and must have had her binoculars trained on us from an upstairs window from early evening. The upshot was that the bulky figure of PC Wing paid various calls, threatening the culprits with an appearance at Mansfield Petty Sessions and pointing out that there was no future in a life of crime.

To make matters worse for me he called at our house, and when he had said his piece he was applauded by my mother. And to prolong the agony he accepted the proffered cup of cocoa and slice of currant cake. Strangely, the signatory to the forbidding notice that had been removed was one of the directors of the firm for which I later went to work and who, with a twinkle in his eye, said my name was still on his file. 'Can't say employing a young criminal would do us much good,' he said, eyeing me over the top of his glasses and controlling the cup he was holding with much difficulty.

Beyond Broom House there was the garage owned for many years by Mr Baden-Powell and it was a common sight to see him off on a breakdown mission, moving with an energy his illustrious namesake would have approved. Those were the days when motoring was not the sophisticated business it is today.

And another thing that was certainly not so sophisticated was the making and receiving of telephone calls. At the side of the Powell garage was a call box, parts of which (and with refinements added no doubt) have stood the test of time, and qualifies it, so I am informed, to be a listed building.

As a young chap newly married, and stationed in Hamburg, it was to that box that I made a call to my wife. Certainly not many private phones about in those days. The year was 1946 and I booked the call from the Salvation Army canteen having arranged with my wife that she would be in the box – she had sent me the number – at a certain time. Far from the slick arrangements we take for granted now the call went: 'Hello Stuttgart, this is Hamburg, a call please to England.' And then: 'Hello Stuttgart, this is Brussels'. And so on, connecting in turn Paris, Calais, Dover, London, Nottingham, finally ringing the phone in the Chapel Street box. A somewhat different arrangement from the day recently when, as a family, we had a three-way call between Leicester, New Zealand and Kirkby, and all talking as though we were seated in the same room!

Opposite the phone kiosk is the entrance to Kirkby House. This imposing residence at one time figured prominently in the Kirkby calendar, particularly at Whitsuntide when the Sunday School scholars traversed the local streets behind brass bands. There were two distinct Whitsuntide Walks, one down at the east end of the town in the morning and ours in the afternoon. Having been a participant for many years it is remembered as a strictly ordered affair. It started with the St Wilfrid's scholars assembling outside the church, with the other Sunday Schools being picked up en route. Were there all that many children you ask? There certainly were. The second contingent, the Baptists, lined up outside their chapel which for years had stood on the area now called Chapel Close. And then, a couple of hundred yards further on, the Wesleyan scholars fell in at the junction of Southwell Lane.

The walk was still not complete: the Park Prims from their tin chapel on Vernon Road were lined up and waiting at the corner of Hampden Street. A few moments' breather while the final lining-up was done and then off the procession went, the Salvation Army Band and – usually – the Kirkby Old Band headed the long lines of children. The walk was on its traditional way. The streets were lined with onlookers; mums, dads, aunts, uncles, grandparents and any number of Kirkby Whitsuntide visitors. And it was all part of the proceedings that watchers would move their vantage points

The streets of Kirkby: deserted here, but never so on Whit Monday.

more than once to see the children and wave to them. Maybe it was the adults' enthusiasm that gave renewed vigour to the children, for the route from start to finish was near enough 2 miles, and 2 miles on a very warm afternoon (and they seem to be the ones remembered) at slow processional pace called for a bit of endeavour.

After the streets had been traversed there was still the saunter through the grounds of Kirkby House where homage had to be paid to Miss Kate Hodgkinson, wealthy benefactress of St Wilfrid's and of much that needed support in the parish. She and her friend Miss Wood sat in front of their beautiful residence in wicker chairs bestowing their nods and occasional waves to the Sunday School scholars.

After the long walk through the west part of the town and the dutiful appearance at Kirkby House there was still the final item on the Monday afternoon agenda. Already scores of grown-ups had assembled for the hymn-singing in the playground of Chapel Street School. With tea only a few lusty verses away the scholars (apart from the very young ones, who were already being well looked after) knew the singing had to be given some real effort, and so 'Come, Holy Ghost, our souls inspire', and 'Come,

Choristers on Victoria Road: part of the Whitsuntide procession.

Further back, school pupils follow.

Returning to church.

thou Holy Spirit, come,' could be a fitting prelude to tea. And you had to let the adults know that you could still sing a bit.

Eventually the children were free to go to their own schoolrooms. Discipline from the teachers was still a factor, but when you had waited for sandwiches, jellies and cream cakes for so long you could manage to wait a bit longer. But my, how good it was to eventually sit down and know that at long last the good things on the tables, mostly supplied by many adults who remembered their own Sunday School days, were treats to which you could give your complete attention.

But there was still one more session to complete the day, and that, you can be sure none of us missed out on. After a couple of hours or so, when you had been home and changed into clothes you didn't have to be quite so careful about, it was off to The Field. It was really Titchfield Park, but it was known as The Field to most of us, certainly on Whit Monday.

It was arranged for one of the bands to turn up and give a concert. That certainly pleased the adults who were there; the musicians, many of whom were miners, had a wide repertoire, and what better way could there be to complete a day steeped in tradition?

For any still-energetic youngsters, games were organised with simple prizes, but it was important to try to win because the honour of your own

The 1928 Whit Walk at the corner of Park Street.

Sunday School was at stake. But it didn't really matter if you hadn't the energy to compete. There was one great finale, simple as it sounds. Mrs Hall, complete with horse and cart, had made the journey up from Mayfield. She was expected, and she never let us down. Her ice cream was delicious, and although it was a treat whenever you bought a cornet from her as she visited various streets on her round throughout the summer, never did it taste better than on Whit Monday evening on The Field. Certainly the bandsmen would agree with that.

And when folk went home, happy and comfortably tired, no doubt there would be a few who looked at the building that had been there for more Whitsuntides than any of us. Tucked comfortably between a house and stone cottages is the old Wesleyan Chapel. Built in 1834 and long since the Mecca for local billiards and snooker players, it no doubt holds countless memories of many Whitsuntides, and has the distinction of giving Chapel Street its name.

18

No Mod Cons

It was not unusual in my very young days for Kirkby families to share a house, so that one family were the tenants and the other family 'had rooms'. All done with the approval of the landlord of course. Research assures me that Kirkby was not the only place where that happened; it was an accepted arrangement throughout the country I am led to believe, certainly in the industrial areas.

We shared 14 Cookson Street with the Cobbs. How the arrangement came about I don't know, but I assume (why did I never ask?) it was the result of friendship. There were five in their family, Mr and Mrs Cobb (Uncle Johnny and Auntie Cobb to me), Bill, Elsie and Leslie. And there were three of us: sister Dorothy was way in the future.

When we moved in with them Bill had already left home, and was on the point of marriage. Did that allow a bit more room? Hardly. The house had a living room, front room, kitchen and pantry downstairs, and upstairs there were front and back bedrooms and an attic. Outside there was a coalhouse, and down at the end of a long garden there was a lavatory and an ashpit; flush lavatories in our area were not generally installed for another four or five years.

Mother, father and I had the front room, use of the kitchen, and the back bedroom. And the pantry of course. But my mother, ever practical, stored much of her provisions in a wooden cupboard in the front room, pushing books that belonged to my father to the back of the shelves.

The heating in the house was entirely by coal. Both the men, Uncle Johnny and my dad, were miners. Johnny worked at the Summit Colliery, which was about three-quarters of a mile away; my Dad worked at Annesley Colliery. Working at Annesley was no picnic; it meant Dad, when he was on days, had to catch the early morning 'paddy' train, coming home late in the afternoon, and when he was on the night shift he caught the late evening 'paddy' and came home about seven the next morning.

Something about the Cobbs. Auntie Cobb (her name was Annie but it was always, at about four years old, Auntie Cobb to me) was a cheerful

soul, of medium height and weighty; Johnny was very small and wiry. Elsie
– I suppose she would be near enough ten years older than me – was a
pleasant girl, never short of companions, and she made a great fuss of me.
Leslie, and I didn't find out about this until much later, was an invalid.
Eventually I was told that he had TB, and I can't remember him ever going
to school. I suspect he slept, on doctor's orders, in the attic. Certainly he
never seemed to spend much time downstairs, and I reckoned, but I
couldn't work things out until much later, that he must have been in his
early teens when he died.

I suppose the Cobbs must have had visits from the doctor, but I was too
young to be brought into that sort of conversation.

I do remember our doctor paying us a visit on one occasion. A
boisterous man, he seemed to fill the room and made himself very much at
home. My mother, I recall, was cooking on the tiny fire. 'And what are we
having for lunch then?' asked the doctor. 'Something smells good.' He was
informed cabbage was being cooked. 'What a lovely colour,' the doctor
said when my mother removed the saucepan lid. 'How do you manage
that?' And Mam said: 'Well you see, Doctor, I always add a pinch of
bicarb.' That was something I remembered and teased her with now and
then.

The lighting in the house was by gas. In the living room the Cobbs had a
light hanging from the ceiling in the middle of the room, and as we were to

Our old-style fireplace.

find later, it gave a reasonable light. Ours, in the front room, was a light fixed to the wall over the fireplace. That too was reasonable, but I do remember it gave off shadows that sometimes frightened me, especially if, for some reason, I had been left on my own temporarily.

Bedtimes were lit by candlelight. There were no light fittings in the bedrooms. Actually I remember feeling more comfortable when the candle was blown out in the bedroom, having first heard my mother's nightly prayer for me said from the bottom of the crib that was placed close to the bed that she and my father shared.

The prayer was the same every night: 'Gentle Jesus, meek and mild, look upon a little child. Pity my simplicity, suffer me to come to Thee.' She then left the room, except on one occasion when I came out with a swear word. It was a word that intrigued me, having heard it spoken by some lad (a relative I suppose) who had visited the Cobbs. My mother was indignant, but kept her cool by saying: 'I don't know where you have heard that, but I do know it was not from my lips, nor from your father's. We (and she emphasised that) don't say words like that.' I was suitably abashed.

Some of the vital household equipment that lived in the shed. The mangle, dolly, chimney brush and, most important of all for my father the miner – the tin bath.

Getting washed wasn't much of a problem for me. I would be accompanied by either my mother or my father, having knocked on the living room door and marched through to the kitchen, but I am sure it was to someone as fastidious as my mother. I would imagine, remembering her, that she would arrange her ablutions when she was sure there was only her and Auntie Cobb in the house. But she always made sure she had a bowl of water kept on the dressing table in the bedroom; it was an arrangement that usually went to plan but there were times when visitors would throw the system out.

But what about the two miners, my father and Uncle Johnny? There were no washing facilities in the mining industry in those long-gone days. That meant colliers came home black. I can only imagine the two men fixed up some sort of arrangement that allowed them in turn to use the kitchen. It was a case of having a bath every day, and that would have to be a time when the bath, hung on the wall by a large iron hook against the coalhouse door, could be brought into the house.

When the grubby mining clothes were due for a wash they were thrown into a staircupboard that was reached via a door off the passage between the front room and the living room, and if the door had been left open you knew the location! The clothes currently in use were kept in a large wooden box in the kitchen divided into two compartments.

On washday there was plenty of water boiled up in the living room fireside boiler, and my mother had to arrange her day with Auntie Cobb. I never remember them falling out over the procedure; it was something they both needed to tackle with common sense, and my mother knew that a good deal depended upon her being able to get a supply of hot water from the boiler when it was needed.

They were great picturegoers, the Cobbs, so there was a fair amount of evening freedom now and then. Mam stuck to her side of the bargain, and we, as a little family, remained (apart from the calls of nature, or if we were going out ourselves) in the front room. We were great readers – happily that was something I took to early – and we added to the gas illumination by a small paraffin lamp.

Each summer, by some means or other, Mam saved enough money for the three of us to have a week's holiday in Skegness. The thrill of that can still be conjured up. It was wonderful, and sometimes we would be joined by an aunt who was 'out service' with a wealthy family in Nottingham. My mother always did the necessary correspondence to get our holiday booked by writing to some address she had been recommended. It was, and I can recall the feeling even now, strange as it may seem, absolutely wonderful to

When the Cobbs were granted alternative accommodation by the council, 14 Cookson Street was ours. Suddenly we seemed to have all the space in the world!

be at the seaside. Simply a different world, with the thrill of building, with Dad's help, sandcastles, having donkey rides, running along the beach.

One magical week in the year. There was nothing like it until the day came when the Cobbs received the great news that they had been granted tenancy of a newly-built council house. Gradually the local council was building and developing small estates as income and facilities allowed. And when that day came and my parents were told they could have the tenancy of 14 Cookson Street the world became a truly different place. There was even talk about the outside toilet arrangements being converted earlier than planned to the flush variety. Would wonders never cease?

But the most marvellous thing was that we suddenly had room, so much room. Even now, at my advanced age, I can remember how excited I was. The room we had lived in for so long was emptied. There was nothing there save an old carpet on the floor. I ran about for the sheer exuberance of having that privilege. It was, it absolutely was, a new exciting world.

19

A Church for All Seasons

A s one would expect of the Mother Church, St Wilfrid's has its own place in the life of Kirkby-in-Ashfield. Like all churches it is unique. The people who worship there – because of their prayers, their fellowship, their interests – make it so. It is a building looked on with affection by those who use it week by week to praise God and thank Him for His goodness. It is part of England's Christian heritage.

A view of St Wilfrid's by Samuel Grimm. He was a friend of Sir Richard Kaye, incumbent from 1765 to 1810.

A morning service in the 1950s.

It is thought there may have been a Saxon church, probably of timber, on the present site, in the seventh century founded by St Wilfrid, but no traces remain to support this claim. But the church is mentioned in the Domesday Book. 'At Cherchbi,' the record states, 'there is a Church and a priest and two mills of three shillings, and three acres of wood meadow and pasture.'

What is certain is that Kirkby, for countless years, was an agricultural village; then, when coal was mined, there was a change, and as time went by that change was accelerated. As more pits were sunk so more work – and workers – came into the industry and settled in the area. The district now has no mines and during the last three decades great industrial and commercial expansion has taken place. East Kirkby and Kirkby-in-Ashfield have taken the latter name to become one town altered almost beyond recognition from the early part of the last century.

Throughout the changing scenes St Wilfrid's has remained a place of inspiration and strength, a large part of its congregation keeping up the family tradition of worshipping there. But the serenity of the village was shattered shortly before midnight on 16 January 1907. A signalman coming off duty from Kirkby Bentinck noticed smoke pouring from the church. It was the start of a fire that would soon envelop the church and leave only the tower and spire without damage.

Nothing could more dramatically convey the situation than the words recorded at the time by the Revd James Butterwick, the rector. He wrote: 'About twenty to twelve the whole place was doomed. Mrs Butterwick was awakened by the roar of the fire, and saw the light of the flames from the bedroom window. She immediately jumped out saying "The church is on fire!" My son was first out of the house, and when I saw the church the whole roof was in flames. All excepting the tower was burned out in two hours. The only thing that was saved was the registers and these were rescued most heroically by Frank Rawson, along with Mr Jewsbury and Mr Oscroft. Frank Rawson drenched himself with water, entered the burning building and brought them out from under the tower.'

The catastrophe to the village was matched by the resolution of the parishioners. Work was started immediately to clear the appalling mess the fire had left, and plans were at once put in place to start the

The scene at St Wilfrid's after the disastrous fire.

A children's fancy dress party on the rectory lawn.

Parishioners preparing for one of the church's acclaimed festivals.

The arrival of the magi, part of a Christmas display at St Wilfrid's.

rebuilding. The local populace made it clear we are told, such had been the love for the church, that the new building should be a replacement of what had been lost. The Diocesan Architect, Mr Louis Ambler, obviously listened to the wishes of the parishioners. Some of the internal furnishings inevitably showed differences, but all were in keeping with the local sentiment.

One of the most wonderful features of the church is the statue of St Wilfrid in a niche over the porch, surely a great tribute to those involved in the restoration work. The oak stalls and pews, and the truly handsome screen are furnishings that cannot fail to impress, and many are the admiring compliments made at the various festivals that in recent years have meant so much to the people involved in the life of the church.

The Manor House, demolished in 1964.

Such were the strenuous efforts after the fire that less than two years later, on 7 November 1908, the church was rededicated and reopened for worship by Dr Edwin Hoskyns, Bishop of Southwell. And now, after the incumbency of some outstanding rectors, the congregations still week by week show their great affection for St Wilfrid's.

With patience, fortitude and determination the seasons are wonderfully represented by the unstinting efforts of teams of flower-arrangers, and it has to be said there have been benefactors whose legacies have helped enormously. Perhaps two should be particularly mentioned: Miss Kate Hodgkinson who lived at Kirkby House in the earlier years of the last century, and Miss Esther Todd whose ongoing bequest still plays a valuable part.

Nowhere could a better insight of village life in the district be made than by studying the sketches made by the artist Samuel Grimm who was a friend of Sir Richard Kaye, incumbent of St Wilfrid's from 1765 to 1810. Grimm was apparently a frequent visitor to the rectory and his drawings illustrate the rural spaciousness of the time. There is special poignancy when one recalls the one-time splendour of the Manor House which was built in 1622 and demolished when Manor House Court was built in 1964.

St Wilfrid's, floodlit for a Christmas service many years ago.

Mention should be made too of the lovely eighteenth-century Kirkby Rectory, now no longer the incumbent's residence. It was sold into private hands some years ago and is mentioned in Nikolaus Pesvner's *Buildings of England*. It has long been accepted locally that there was an underground passage from the rectory to the Duke of Wellington public house on Church Street. A former licensee of the Duke tells of inspecting the passage, but confirms it was sealed thirty years ago; and with the sealing went the story of it being used for nefarious land tax activities by local squires.

20

Two Tin Chapels

We called them tin chapels, but that was because we tried to be a bit uppity. The places some of us went to – St Wilfrid's, the Wesleyan Methodist or Chapel Street Baptist – were solid buildings of stone or brick. But it should be made clear at the outset: the atmosphere the tin chapels (they were actually corrugated iron) generated was deeply religious and their congregations were regular in attendance and devotions. The adults were, anyway; there are not all that many saints among children – certainly not in a collection of them aged between five and fifteen.

Vernon Road Chapel was for years the home of the young Park Prims (but Primitive Methodists when on their best behaviour and under the watchful eye of diminutive Mr Brown, his much taller wife and daughter, or in the sometimes stern but humble presence of Danny Pickering). The Park had a sizeable Sunday School, drawn mainly from the top of Cookson Street to the bottom of Vernon Road and the streets leading off. But either side of the place itself were families whose allegiance to another place of worship was unshakeable. Next door to the chapel on one side were the Shooters, and on the other side lived Kemps and various of the large Grice clan. Sunday by Sunday the Shooters, Kemps and Grices could be found striding out to join other Wesleyan Methodists, pillars of an establishment that has weathered the years. Sunday, I seem to remember, was the one day when Mr Kemp left his bicycle at home. On the other six days of the week he could be seen awheel, pedalling just enough to keep the machine in motion, and paying constant attention to the mirror fixed high on his handlebars.

The chapel on Vernon Road was built around the turn of the twentieth century, and for more than seventy years served its small but stout-hearted handful of members who struggled to maintain attendances. Its greatest years, perhaps, were those leading up to and just after the Second World War. Congregations then were very often enough to fill the wooden benches, and many a distinguished cleric preached with a sincerity that held more than a hundred spellbound. Some of the Sunday-by-Sunday sermons were probably a bit long, but maybe the preacher for the day had travelled a considerable distance, and a ten-minute stint would hardly justify his journey. There were no small screens and carefully-timed programmes then to cause unseemly fidgeting and barely concealed glances at watches; so, if you had banked the fire up well at home there was hardly a better place to be. You might miss a bit of Reginald Foort playing the BBC organ, but you would be home in time to hear Albert Sandler and his musicians at half-past eight. In the meantime you could join fifty or sixty other worshippers in a rousing end to the evening as you sang the last hymn accompanied by the harmonium.

For a time there was a devoted band of adults who gave unstintingly of their leisure time and hard-earned cash to enable the little chapel to be kept in a good state of repair. Pickerings, Browns, Hardwicks, Wallises, Bradfords, Atkins: they would be there on Sunday evenings, and turn up at some time during the week to do what jobs were necessary. To save expense it had to be 'do-it-yourself', although that expression was way into a future few contemplated.

Through the week there was a simple steadfastness that expressed itself in faith teas, Band of Hope meetings, Bible classes, Ladies' Bright Hours; and every now and then someone with a special gift for mass

Drawn from memory, remembered with affection. Both chapels were very similar.

communication would lead Revivalist Weekends, with a call to repentance to waverers young and old. The words of fire suddenly gave way to hushed tones as the evangelist exhorted the hesitant to accept 'The Keys to the Kingdom', and then it became unbearably moving as the congregation sang reverently to provide a fitting background.

But there were often concerts (mainly on Saturday evenings) when young and not so young recited or sang – good singers, too, some of the adults, offering a talent little suspected – and, after a solid hour or so there would be sandwiches, ginger beer and cakes. And then you felt you could lean back and take the second half, with your tie loosened and the contented feeling that always accompanied the realisation that tomorrow was Sunday, and real school didn't start again until Monday morning.

Was there the same approach at the Bentinck Tin Chapel? That place of worship was neighbour to the railway station, on a piece of land at the top of Princess Street, and there were times when devotions were interrupted by trains clanking past in either direction. (Not that they all clanked; some main-line expresses hurtled through to keep to the tight schedules for which the 'namers' were famous.)

Understandably, some of the district's churches and chapels attracted many of their worshippers from the same families. It was certainly the case at Kirkby Bentinck. The McMurdos were as involved as any family could be, and there were enough relatives, counting those who claimed their right through marriage, to make up a sizeable congregation on their own. And it wasn't as though they lived on the chapel doorstep.

Arthur and Cecil McMurdo were near neighbours on Wilson Avenue, and each Sunday morning, rain or shine, could be seen striding out soon after nine o'clock, to walk the best part of a mile and a half to be in attendance at the Sunday School. Back home they would walk when school and the morning service were over, only to set out again for their second visit of the day after an early tea. Arthur, close to 6ft tall, barrel-chested, and a long-time servant of the Mansfield and Sutton CWS, died a comparatively young man; brother Cecil continued the Sunday walking ritual until the Bentinck Chapel closed, then joined the Hill Methodists, his faith undiminished through his remaining years.

There could be few families who presented a more united front than the McMurdos, and for years they took holidays together camping in a village just over the Derbyshire border. The womenfolk and children spent much of the summer school holidays there, to be joined by the men at the weekends. And, to those who knew them, it would come as no surprise to learn that part of the family Sundays were given over to divine service, with one of their number preaching to his captive congregation.

Amos Briggs was brother-in-law to the family and a well-known local preacher, and on his day a good one. But, like so many of his persuasion, he could go on a bit when the inspiration drove him. When he was taking the camping service on one particular Sunday there came an audible whisper from one of the congregation as he rose to preach. 'I'll give him twenty minutes to do his stuff and then I'm going to light my pipe!'

The Bentinck Chapel closed in 1966 after an adjustment in the local Methodist Circuit, and the land, acquired by the first members from the Colliery Company at about the same time as the Vernon Road Chapel was being built, was marked for housing development. By the time of the closure the membership had dwindled but, like Cecil McMurdo, the stalwarts who were left transferred their allegiance to enrich other devoted groups.

There were periods in the chapel's sixty-five year history when services were continuously well attended, and at Whitsuntide (when the scholars did their own Whit Walk) and on Anniversary Sundays the place was full to bursting. The little chapel fitted unobtrusively into the working life of the neighbourhood, offering fellowship and spiritual refreshment to those who felt the need.

21

Winter & Teatime Toast

Ifirst knew the walk in my childhood – and that is a good many years ago – so I decided, seeing the world has changed a bit since those days, to set out again and see if my legs would last out. In our part of Nottinghamshire one stretch of the route (and that has been mentioned somewhere else in these reminiscences) is 636ft above sea level we were always told at school. One thing for sure, whatever the height, it could be bitingly cold. I reminded myself of that when I set out from Kirkby's Four Lane Ends.

I don't suppose all that much has altered on the long pull up Diamond Avenue: Forest Hill is the name that sticks with many of the locals, but breathing becomes a bit more laboured with the passing years. A steady pace is called for, and with perseverance fifteen to twenty minutes should take you far enough over the top to see the lie of the land towards distant Larch Farm. That well-known landmark must be close on 2 miles away but we shall be turning well short of that at the traffic lights where the road dips.

At the turn you have most of the next mile to yourself apart from an almost unbroken chain of vehicles going both ways. Drivers will be carefully watching the road; isolated pedestrians must obviously have somewhere in mind to be out and about on a cold winter day. Well, that is a fair assumption. It never was very busy with walkers but in my youth there were certainly likely to be more about than now. There was a seat placed up to the hedgerow but I can't imagine there would be much call for sitting, I told myself as I strode on. I noted that there was little activity at the turn to Hollinwell Golf Club. No doubt there would have been keen players somewhere on the course earlier in the day, and doubtless they would have reason to make a judicious call to sample the comforts of the clubhouse before leaving.

Over in a field not far from Hollinwell were a few caravans, symbol of country lovers, neatly placed and far from the madding crowd. And over to my right I passed the meadow where there have been from time to time

Late winter at Winshaw Well Farm.

summer sounds of the latest in the swinging world of music will be made to the delight of enthusiastic crowds.

On I walked, eager now to get a close look at Winshaw Well Farm. It was to the spot my mother referred, seventy years ago, when she said: 'Right. When you are feeling ready my lad we shall set off on our walk round the duckpond.' To be truthful I can't recall seeing any ducks there but she stoutly defended seeing one or two splashing about in her young days.

On this day I looked carefully at the now beautifully sited farmstead, wonderfully improved, and I made a special point of looking for the pond. And there it is, close to the roadside hedge and in keeping with the layout, even boasting its own tiled wellhouse.

While I paused long enough to take in Winshaw Well I thought back to the one-time owners of the farm. They were the Newton family, well-known and respected throughout Kirkby. They lived there for many years. I didn't know them well enough to record much of their activities; being so far out of the growing township they would no doubt be glad to rest when their busy day's labour was done.

But many of my family knew Mrs Newton: she was a regular whenever possible at distant St Wilfrid's Church – what a trip that would be in those far gone days – and was particularly enthusiastic about attending the Mothers' Union monthly meetings, often arriving in one of the farm vehicles. She was a fervent Christian lady and each day when she was able she listened to the Morning Prayer on the radio. And when it came to the part of the service inviting listeners to pray she would kneel by the side of her table and reverently follow the broadcast on her knees.

It was pleasant to pause for a few moments, but not too long. On such a walk I find it necessary to keep to the steady rhythm of my strides. Stopping and starting can turn out to be a wearisome business for legs that

A view of the wellhouse and now-splendid pond.

The highest point in Nottinghamshire the plaque informs us: 609ft above sea level.

are getting on a bit. So on I went, keen now to see the stretch of road where at one time – but a long time ago – there stood a restaurant on the very brow of the Shoulder of Mutton Hill.

Hard to believe now, but most certainly the restaurant was a one-time local landmark and there is a photograph to prove it. What a trade it might have done had it still been there. But I didn't stop; the place I wanted to check was the plaque above the door of one of the neat row of houses. I had seen it countless times from my car but this day I thought I should satisfy myself by taking a note of the inscription. I did: it told the world quite simply that this was (and no doubt still is) the highest point in Nottinghamshire in the year 1904, and informing the curious that it is 609ft above sea level. People from Huthwaite's Strawberry Bank might dispute the highest claim, but how satisfying it was to stand beneath the plaque for a minute or two while I recorded the details.

After duly noting the information I turned at the peak of the Shoulder of Mutton Hill; and how accurate that name is bearing in mind its position and the long curve of the hill as you start your trudge back to the town.

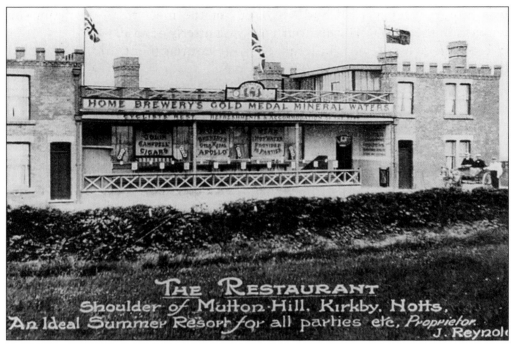

The one-time restaurant, in its day an inviting stop.

You have before you a goodish walk still to get back to where you started at the Four Lane Ends: near enough a mile, and making the round trip a good 3 miles.

I think back to the days when cars for most folk were a luxury well into the future, and to start from our old house in Cookson Street you would need to add another mile each way.

Recalling that I can so well remember the occasion when the walk was done (my sister was too young and was company for my father, resting a while before the morrow's labour) striding out with my mother. And how well that dear lady could tramp in her prime.

But there was delight as soon as we reached home. Dad had poked up the fire to send streamers of light and warmth across the room. The delight was compounded when the gas was lit and the curtains drawn.

Then the table was set. Home-made bread, thick enough to toast when the fire was going well. Blackcurrant jam and Mam's home-made scones to follow. We took our plates close to the fire, two of us sneaking an extra bit of butter before spreading the jam. My cheeks would be glowing still and I was hungry. Henry Hall and his band set the meal to music from the wireless in the corner. For an hour you were utterly at ease.

To walk 5 miles you had earned your contentment and that added deliciously to the simple winter meal.

22

Three Large Dogs

It had been a most luxurious bath, I remember, following a September Sunday's toil in the garden. As I towelled myself I looked forward to utter relaxation in front of *Sunday Night Theatre*. But my leisurely towelling was interrupted. There was a hurried tapping on the bathroom door. 'Oh, what is it?' I asked with some irritation. 'There's someone downstairs to see you,' whispered Doris. 'Who?' I asked, adopting a conspiratorial tone.

'Come on, make haste,' she said. 'Don't keep him waiting.' And away she went.

I hurried, annoyed. Visitors are usually welcome, but there are times when you have mentally adjusted yourself to snugness and complete seclusion.

But one must be sociable. By the time I had put on a clean shirt and brushed my hair I was feeling more friendly, and on the point of entering the sitting room, I was, if not actually radiating love and goodwill, perfectly affable.

I opened the door: in front of the fire was a dog. On either side of the fireplace were grinning humans.

This brute, then, seeming to cover about half the room area, was the someone to see me. I had hurried my towelling and quelled frustration for a cross between an Alsatian and a Greyhound. And all I got was a look-over by a limpid and rather appealing eye.

The elder boy and his Nana, it seems, had been followed by this dog to evening service. Leaving him at the church porch they had found him waiting for them when the service was over. This time the animal refused to be shaken off, and here he was, stretched out on our best carpet.

To appeal to the most accessible side of the dog's nature he was supplied with liquid and food, and then coaxed along to the police station. He was very reluctant to leave his benefactors; I, for several weeks, was rather reluctant to take a bath on Sunday evenings. I was also very reluctant, following a bout of unarmed combat with a huge (I'm sure it was huge) brindled mongrel, to sit on the back seat of a car.

We were having alterations done in the kitchen, and the old fellow whose men were doing the job came along to see how things were going. I happened to mention I wanted a few slates for a bit of re-roofing on the garage. He invited me to go along with him to his yard.

We went out to his car. Occupying the front passenger seat sat the mongrel. The builder held up a restraining hand as I was about to enter the vehicle. 'Don't try to get in until I do. If you do my old pal there will have you.'

He grinned and screwed himself into the driving seat.

When we had gone about a hundred yards the builder said: 'I want to make a call before we go to the yard.' The significance of that did not strike me, but it was not lost on our brindled friend, apparently, for as soon as the builder had slammed the car door behind him and departed on his errand, I found myself staring into a pair of hostile canine eyes.

Just making sure there are no dogs about!

Well-known builder Mr Hitchin in the doorway surveying work in progress. His dog was no doubt guarding his car!

The builder's words 'My old pal will have you' seemed about to come true. The dog must have sensed I was easy meat. But, although not willing to try for the initiative, I was not prepared to succumb without hoisting my defences. It was a roomy car, and I swung up my feet until the soles of my gardening boots were no more than a whisker's width from the twitching muzzle.

Thus we stayed, a back-seat passenger in a builder's car acrobatically poised and passing a very unhealthy five minutes.

The builder returned, and the four-footed guardian turned docilely to stare through the windscreen, having prevented me running nimbly off with a hundredweight bag of cement under each arm.

The episode of the third dog also concerns a car and a back seat. But this time our little family car and a strange, but friendly dog. The car, freshly cleaned, stood in the roadway. I, the weekend chauffeur, bade the family take their places. They trooped out of the gate and I held the nearside door open.

Before the younger child could occupy his rightful place a dog, hitherto loping at a fair trot along the pavement, swerved and entered the car. Not only did it enter, but it lay, full length, on the back seat.

The kids simply loved it. Doris ordered me to remove the dog. But that was easier said than done, and fifteen precious minutes of a sunny summer afternoon had gone before the animal could be persuaded to leave. My entreaties met with no success, and I was wondering what to do next when the dog nonchalantly ambled down from the seat and in a moment was once more off on his loping run. Maybe he had been a little early for an appointment and had found our car a welcome, if temporary, haven.

Three dogs, then; perhaps a little surprising that none of them was shaggy.

Acknowledgements

I am grateful to the following for their assistance in compiling this book.

The drawings on pages 2 and 68 were kindly supplied by the Paragon Press. (All other drawings are by the author.)

Grateful thanks for permission to reproduce photographs go to the PDD of St Wilfrid's Church, to Sylvia Sinfield and the many people whose kindness and co-operation has made possible the Old Kirkby Collection.

Special thanks go to Frank Ashley for his expertise in producing CDs and many photographic prints in preparation for the publication of this book.